Susan Marg has a B.A in social psychology from Cornell University and a MSc in a market research from Boston University. She derived her interest in history from her husband. She grew up in Cleveland, Ohio and she has a Mindwesterner's easy going, friendly disposition that even 15 years living on the East coast and working in the telecommunications industry couldn't quell. Susan now lives in Arizona where it is hot.

Susan's first book was *Las Vegas weddings: A brief history, Celebrity Gossip, Everything Elvis, and the compalete Chapel Guide.*

It is filled with Vegas Iore and mixed with Hollywood tales of love and marriage and the subsequent fallout.

To the children of Desert Shadow Elementary School in
Paradise Valley, Arizona. May you always feel
empowered and achieve your dreams.

Susan Marg

EMPOWERED LADIES

A Trip in Pants Through History

AUSTIN MACAULEY PUBLISHERS™

LONDON • CAMBRIDGE • NEW YORK • SHARJAH

Copyright © Susan Marg 2024

All rights reserved. No part of this publication may be reproduced, distributed, or transmitted in any form or by any means, including photocopying, recording, or other electronic or mechanical methods, without the prior written permission of the publisher, except in the case of brief quotations embodied in critical reviews and certain other non-commercial uses permitted by copyright law. For permission requests, write to the publisher.

Any person who commits any unauthorized act in relation to this publication may be liable to criminal prosecution and civil claims for damages.

The story, the experiences, and the words are the author's alone.

Ordering Information
Quantity sales: Special discounts are available on quantity purchases by corporations, associations, and others. For details, contact the publisher at the address below.

Publisher's Cataloging-in-Publication data
Marg, Susan
Empowered Ladies

ISBN 9798891552005 (Paperback)
ISBN 9798891552012 (ePub e-book)

Library of Congress Control Number: 2023922378

www.austinmacauley.com/us

First Published 2024
Austin Macauley Publishers LLC
40 Wall Street, 33rd Floor, Suite 3302
New York, NY 10005
USA

mail-usa@austinmacauley.com
+1 (646) 5125767

Table of Contents

Introduction

Introduction to Empowered Ladies

Being empowered does not necessarily have a happy ending. Or beginning or middle. Some women who wore pants lived in fear of being found out. If they enlisted in early wars as men, (and only men were allowed to enlist), they were afraid that they would be sent home in shame.

When Billy Tipton, the jazz musician, died, the world was amazed when it was learned that he was a she. She had lived as a man her adult life. When Dr. James Barry, a surgeon who rose to the highest medical position in the British Army, was found out upon his death, the army covered it up.

They weren't all ladies, but they certainly were of the female persuasion. They were women who went against societal expectations. Sometimes, they wore pants or disguised themselves in other ways as men.

They included saints and sinners, queens, countesses, and common folks. You might be familiar with some of them, such as Calamity Jane and Joan of Arc. Still, their stories are complex.

Introduction to Part 1

This book focuses on Western Civilization, particularly in the United States. It looks at women's fashions from Ancient Egypt through the 1980s. It takes a look at which women went against society's norms and why.

In some of the following sections in Part 1 are women who participated in the American Revolution, the Civil War, World War I, and World War II. More women are included in other sections. Changes brought about in women's clothing, such as through sports, and the Wild West are examined. There are also myths that are told, as well as stories about nuns and queens, slaves, and pirates. Over time, laws concerning cross-dressing have changed. Even today, we continue to see changes.

There has been one constant throughout centuries of women's fashions. Women did not wear pants. World events began to change that, but not until the mid-1850s when the women's trousers movement was linked to the women's rights movement.

Throughout history, women were considered the weaker sex in need of protection. Roman women were not allowed to own property or control their own finances, nor could they vote. In early America, they were expected to get married, have children, work at home, and obey their husbands. In the 1950s, women were still treated as second-class citizens, even though they could vote. A world war changed that.

There were also US cities that banned women from wearing pants as part of anti-cross-dressing laws until well into the twentieth century. These included Detroit and Miami that made such laws in the late 1950s. There was also San Francisco, Columbus, Chicago, and Houston, as well as others.

Was there a collective sigh of relief? In 2013, the French government overturned a ban on women wearing pants in Paris. It had been on the books for over two hundred years and ignored. More than a fashion statement, it was designed to keep women from certain jobs. Pants had also become a symbol of the French Revolution.

Pants were eventually adopted by men and women because they were practical and comfortable, particularly on horseback. They protected the legs and kept the wearer covered while allowing for easy movement.

Clothes have always been a symbol of wealth. It set those apart from having to do manual labor, even housework, that might damage a garment. In addition to having a variety of dresses, attention to detail, and the material itself demonstrated differences between classes. This was less true of men as men's fashion changed little over time.

In Ancient Egypt, no one wore pants—it was just too hot. Men wore garments that were simply constructed. Noblemen wore a wraparound skirt and a top. The pants were usually belted.

Women wore straight full-length dresses with one or two straps over the shoulder. Dresses were pleated or draped. Women's clothing was more conservative than men's.

Ancient Romans and Greeks thought pants were barbaric because they associated them with those outside their culture, particularly with the Germanic tribes. In fact, in Rome, in 397 AD, pants were declared illegal. The ban was repeated declaring that the wearer be punished and expelled. There was no particular hygienic reason for the ban.

In the Middle Ages, pants were part of a knight's uniform. Thereafter, they were associated with men, a symbol of strength.

In 1820 and later, trousers were in general use among men. Before then, they wore breeches, made of buckskin for daily wear or silk for the evening. They covered the body from the waist with separate coverings for each leg. These went out of favor when men adopted trousers.

There were also knickers, baggy-kneed breeches, and pantaloons. Pantaloons were only recommended for men whose legs were slim and muscular.

Baseball players historically wore a stylized form of knickerbockers.

Why did some women dress as men? Reasons, of which there are many, vary with the circumstances. Hatshepsut, Queen Pharaoh of Egypt, wanted to maintain power. During the war, the American Revolution or the Civil War, for example, some women were patriotic.

Some jobs simply could not be done in a long skirt. Charley Parkhurst was a stagecoach driver. Billy Tipton wanted to travel with a band and play jazz. And no one told George Sand what to do.

Section 1.1
Birth of the United States

During the American Revolution, most women were noncombatants, but they were subjected to the consequences of war, including suffering, violence, and death. Still, they put their skills to use in a variety of important ways. Some women sewed uniforms, clothes, and blankets for soldiers. Some made bullets, as well as rolled and packed cartridges. Others raised funds for the war effort.

The women struggled to maintain their homesteads as fighting raged nearby. Rape by the enemy troops was always a possibility and a source of fear for women defending their homes alone.

Women joined army regiments for various reasons: fear of starvation, rape, loneliness, and imminent poverty—either as a last resort or to follow their husbands.

Wives of some officers visited the camps frequently. Martha Washington was often with her husband at Valley Forge, where she also served as a nurse to injured soldiers.

Other patriotic women concealed army dispatches and letters containing sensitive military information underneath their petticoats as they rode through enemy territory to deliver it.

Nancy Morgan Hart, a passionate Patriot, stayed on the farm with her children when her husband enlisted on the Patriots' side. She was built for the task, both physically and emotionally. To match her height being six foot tall, red-headed, and muscular, she had a feisty personal demeanor. She had also grown up on the family farm where she was required to work hard to keep the family fed, clothed, and safe. She had a hotheaded temper and a penchant for exacting vengeance upon those who offended her or her family and friends. Although illiterate, she had the skills necessary for frontier survival as she was an expert herbalist, a skilled hunter, and an excellent shooter.

A favorite story, there is little documentation, has Nancy outwitting a group of Tories who had invaded her home to spy on her. She served them wine with food, as they demanded. When they were drunk, she took their weapons, killing two and holding the others until help arrived. She displayed legend and inspiration, the traditionally masculine skills of hunting, farming, fishing, and repair work.

Following the war, Nancy disguised herself as a 'touched' or as an emotionally disturbed man, to obtain intelligence on British defenses. Her mission was such a success that during the Civil War, a group of women banded together to form a militia unit in her honor, illustrating how her legacy has survived.

Only sixteen years old, Sybil Ludington was a female Paul Revere, best known for his midnight ride to alert the colonial militia as to the approach of British forces.

Ludington rode forty miles in the rain and also at night to rouse troops about the British. Unfortunately, no contemporary accounts exist, but she was considered a hero by many.

Although there was no official organization, there were also women spies, on both sides, during the American Revolution. They were considered too simple to understand strategy, and they could pass through checkpoints without raising suspicion.

Hannah Blair was one such woman. A Quaker by birth, she wanted to support the Patriots. She helped not only with food, supplies, and medicine but also mended uniforms and carried messages. She is also given credit for saving the lives of two soldiers, by hiding them with the corm as she continued shucking. The Tories continued to search for them. She was caught and forced to watch while her farmhouse was burned down.

After the war, the new government gave Blair formal thanks and a small pension for her wartime service.

Section 1.2
Civil War, a Divided Nation

It was difficult for women during the Civil War, too. Many women followed both the northern and southern armies. They served soldiers and officers as washerwomen, cooks, nurses, seamstresses, and occasionally soldiers and spies.

A woman might also be a camp follower, who received a small wage and was supplied with a half ration of food for herself. Camp followers' duties were primarily the same as other women although the term was often used in a derogatory manner.

In the mid-1800s and during the Civil War, women were expected to comport themselves properly, even when well-dressed in an ensemble that could weigh up to fifteen pounds, once petticoats, corsets, and yards of fabric were counted. To help those who needed help to know what to do, there was *the Ladies' Guide to Perfect Gentility in Manners, Dress, and Conversation*, published in 1854. It included such tips pertaining to:

Having bad breath;
Avoiding freckles;
Managing long skirts:

When tripping over the pavement, a lady should gracefully raise her dress a little above her ankle.

With your right hand, hold together the folds of your gown, and draw them toward the right side.

It also noted that raising the dress on both sides and with both hands was vulgar. This was only to be tolerated when the mud was very deep.

Sarah Edmonds was one of many (the exact number is not known, but it is estimated to be between 250 and 500) who began to change the perception of women in battle. Edmonds adopted a male alias to escape an unwanted marriage.

Changing her appearance was the easy part. Still, Sarah needed to act on the part, as well. It was easier for her than other young women as she had grown up on a farm and she had not been as bothered about learning the ins and outs of how ladies move and sit as most city girls would have been. She was used to walking through the forest and across fields in long, loping, athletic strides and riding astride rather than side saddle, and she loved the outdoors.

Despite her small stature, none suspected she was a woman. She was clever and daring. Like her male comrades, she was often more than tired, yet did extraordinary work. She was unwilling to be outdone by the other men and was often exposed to fire.

She was shot in the thigh in battle. To hide her true identity, she pried the bullet out of her leg with her bare hands. When an illness later in the year led to her regiment's doctor learning this information anyway, he kept her secret until she was to be discharged at the end of the war.

Without question, Sarah was accepted as a good soldier. Her efforts were acknowledged by her peers as well as by her government. She spent long hours in the saddle. It was dangerous work because of Southern sympathizers. For her wartime efforts, she received a government pension.

She claimed that she also served as a Union spy, going behind enemy lines. She disguised herself as a slave boy, an Irish peddler woman, and a Confederate soldier. This has been accepted in popular culture, but some academics and historians dispute this as fact.

In later life, she married, had children, wrote her memoirs, and went on the lecture circuit.

Mary Edwards Walker was many things: an abolitionist, prohibitionist, prisoner of war, and surgeon. She received the Medal of Honor for all she did. She was frequently arrested for wearing men's clothing. She always insisted that she had the right to dress as she pleased and believed appropriate.

Walker grew up on a farm, nor did she wear women's clothing as she worked, feeling it was too restrictive and unhealthy.

At the outbreak of the Civil War, she volunteered as a surgeon, but she was rejected by the army for her gender. She next applied to the Union Army as a civilian. At first, she could only practice as a nurse.

She was arrested by Confederate troops for being a spy and imprisoned, refusing to wear the clothing provided to her.

She never gave up on reforming women's dress.

There are many women whose names have been forgotten over time. Cathay Williams was a black woman who posed as a man and enlisted in the army under a false name. Loreta Janeta Velazquez, a Cuban by birth, did also. She wrote that she had masqueraded as a male Confederate soldier during the Civil War although the first of her four husbands was against the ploy.

Section 1.3
World War I, a Deadly Conflict

World War I strengthened the suffrage movement as more women entered the labor force. They worked in shipyards, foundries, and factories. They wore trousers, tunics, and turbans. When driving tractors, they wore breeches. They donated their corsets to yield 28,000 pounds of steel.

Female factory workers started wearing overalls; women in public services used a uniform similar to a suit with long trousers in winter. That women had to wear male clothes was, however, not seen as a transgression of gender boundaries. It was rather regarded as a convenient occurrence during wartime.

Over time, specific designs tailored to the practical needs of female industrial workers were developed.

Remember that the axiom at the time was 'A woman's place is in the home'. Great lengths were taken to assure the nation that women would not become 'masculinized' by stepping outside of their traditional roles and stepping into jobs traditionally held by men—the men who were now marching off to war.

Although not permitted to fight, women were everywhere.

Eight million women volunteered as American Red Cross workers in a variety of capacities. They made surgical dressings, masks, and gowns, operated servicemen's canteens to provide wholesome entertainment for soldiers and sailors, volunteered as nurse's aides in veterans' hospitals, and provided recreational services to convalescing servicemen. Nearly twenty thousand nurses were provided to the Army, Navy, and US Health Service by the Red Cross.

Those who could drive provided transportation to canteens, hospitals, and camps, both at home and overseas. Seven thousand women worked as 'Hello Girls'—switchboard operators working for the US Army Signal Corps. There were 1,100 librarians at home and abroad supplying books and periodicals to American service members. The Army and Navy Nurse Corps contributed 22,804 nurses to the war effort, serving at home, abroad, and on hospital and troop ships. Although women did not yet have the right to vote, they showed that they had the right stuff.

Even President Woodrow Wilson after the war was convinced that women had earned the right to vote—they were patriots.

The automobile age was just getting underway in World War I, and motorized ambulances became key to medical treatment on the battlefield. Many women who knew how to drive volunteered to go overseas to serve as drivers or mechanics.

Marie Curie was the first person to win or share two Nobel Prizes. She discovered polonium and radium, championed the use of radiation, and fundamentally changed our understanding of radioactivity. During the war, she realized that wounded soldiers were better treated immediately and saw a need for radiological centers near the front lines. She did a quick study of radiology, anatomy, and automotive mechanics; procured X-ray equipment, vehicles, and generators; and developed such units. It is estimated that over a million soldiers were treated with her X-ray unit.

She had to overcome barriers in both Poland, her native country, and France, her adopted country, because she was a woman. Still, after the war, the French government awarded her a stipend for her work. She was only sixty-six years old when she died, presumably from the effects of radiation, which were not known at the time.

Dorothy Lawrence was an English reporter, who posed as a man to report on the front lines during World War I. She went to France and managed to obtain a military uniform and a false identity. She cut her hair to the military style, which was very short, darkened her complexion with shoe polish, and used cotton and wool to extend her shoulders. She learned to drill and march. Upon entering the war zone, she was arrested. She was interrogated as a spy or a prostitute and sent home.

Mata Hari, her stage name, was on the other side. An exotic dancer, she was convicted of spying for Germany and executed by a French firing squad.

Section 1.4
World War II, a Global Conflict

World War II was similar for women as World War I.

Those on the home front, of which there were nineteen million women, did their bit: they contributed to food conservation, Liberty Bond drives, and general community activities, such as planting gardens and canning produce. They donated blood and sent care packages where needed. Women did not wear stockings. They went barelegged, as nylon was not widely available. To conserve fabric, skirts were shorter, and silhouettes were slimmer.

Like Rosie the Riveter, more than six million women took jobs in factories in World War II. Another three million volunteered with the Red Cross.

During World War II, approximately 350,000 US women served with the armed forces. As many as 543 died in war-related incidents, including sixteen nurses who were killed by enemy fire—even though US political and military leaders had decided not to use women in combat because they feared public opinion.

There were no women in armed conflict. They were not allowed. Still, they were often near the front lines, often in danger.

More than 60,000 army nurses (all military nurses were women at the time) served stateside and overseas during World War II. Although most were kept far from combat.

In addition, more than 14,000 Navy nurses served stateside, overseas on hospital ships, and as flight nurses.

Several hundred women were recruited from colleges to take part in the Manhattan Project that built the atomic bomb. They worked as engineers, technicians, and mathematicians throughout the whole project.

Five million women entered the workforce between 1940 and 1945. The gap in the labor force created by departing soldiers meant opportunities for women.

Women also served as spies for the Office of Strategic Services (OSS), a United States intelligence agency. Of the 4,500 women employed by the OSS as clerks, operations agents, codebreakers, and undercover agents, 1,500 worked overseas.

Virginia Hall, an American, had a prosthetic leg. That did not stop her as she worked for the American Office of Strategic Services (OSS) and Britain's clandestine service. She became an expert in organizing resistance movements, supplying agents with money, and helping downed airmen to escape.

She fled France to avoid capture by the Germans but then returned as a wireless operative. She worked in German-occupied territory and continued her work. She was the first woman to take up residence in France, living behind enemy lines, and she is considered to be the most successful American spy.

Jane Kendeigh was a Navy nurse. Landing on Iwo Jima with other flight nurses, they evacuated and tended to the wounded and sick. She was the first naval flight nurse to fly to an active combat zone.

Nancy Harkness Love was the first female pilot in the Army Air Forces. She also founded and commanded a group of female pilots that ferried supplies from factories to air bases. Before the war, she worked as a test and commercial pilot alongside her husband. At the end of the war, Love and her husband were decorated simultaneously.

Ruby Bradley entered the US Army Nurse Corps (ANC) as a surgical nurse. When she retired with the rank of Colonel, she was one of the most decorated women in US military history. Only three weeks after the bombing of Pearl Harbor, she was captured and held in a concentration camp, interned with prisoners of war. She immediately began providing medical attention to other prisoners, smuggled food to those who needed it, and often went hungry to make sure others didn't. She lost so much weight that she was able to smuggle outdated medical equipment and supplies into the camp by hiding them under her clothes, without raising suspicion. She also served during the Korean War.

Whether receiving medals, ribbons, or other decorations, there were so many others who made a difference.

Section 1.5
Oh, Dear, What to Wear

Going back to the 1850s, early women's rights advocates, such as Elizabeth Cady Stanton and Susan B. Anthony, adopted bloomers. This might be, but any woman in the middle of the century had to be very brave if they wore bloomers as they faced much ridicule. Bloomers were considered to be very radical.

In the 1850s, women wore dresses with large, voluminous skirts, and men wore suits with dark coats and light trousers. Women's skirts became increasingly large throughout the decade, a trend supported by the introduction of the crinoline, a structured undergarment created with hoops. No wonder bloomers were not appreciated by the masses.

Bloomers were divided into women's outer garments for the lower body. They were viewed as a healthful and comfortable alternative to the heavy, constrictive dresses worn by American women. They also allowed for unrestricted movement and greater freedom. There were various versions. One of the more popular styles consisted of a short skirt and pants, resembling a Turkish dress.

When introduced to the new style, Amelia Bloomer announced to the readers of her journal that she was the first female to own, operate, and edit a newspaper for women she had adopted the costume herself and printed a description with instructions on how to make it. Soon after, it was called The 'Bloomer' dress.

In the 1890s, an updated version was introduced for athletic use, particularly bicycling. Still, the public was not ready although it was a time of change. While men still wore three-piece suits, the comfort and practicality of looser cuts slowly started to replace more formal options. Women's fashion followed the same trend. Dresses focused more on mobility, with free-flowing skirts. Freedom of movement and expression were valued.

Parisian women were wearing bloomers because the clothing was presented as a fashion item, rather than a political one, such as one for women's rights.

British women became interested in bloomers after delegates to an international peace conference wore them.

By the 1900s, more change was underway, thanks to the typewriter, telephone, post office, camera, sewing machine, and new fabrics. Factory work was often unsafe and harsh with long hours and required more appropriate clothing.

By the 1920s and 1930s, women increasingly wore trousers for leisurewear, as well as comfort, fashion, and work.

With the crash of 1929, flappers dropped out of style, too. Gone was the boyish look, the flapper dress with its straight silhouette, no sleeves, and plunging neckline. Forget skirts above the knee or knee-length, rather scandalous for the time. Even bobbed hair disappeared. Fashion was much more conservative.

Fashions continue to change because people change, influenced by popular culture, be they in the movies, sports, or the radio. Katharine Hepburn and other Hollywood beauties liked wearing pants.

After World War I, Coco Chanel pioneered women's pants. In the 1920s, the French fashion designer created trousers for herself to make it easier to climb into the rocking gondolas in Venice. Her wide trousers for all leisure activities also displayed a certain elegance.

During the second wave of feminism in the 1960s and 1970s, women's trousers finally gained acceptability in the workplace. Several state laws in America declared it unlawful for employers to deny workers the right to wear pants based on their sex.

Yves Saint Laurent introduced the pantsuit in 1967. As he once noted, "I've always wanted to give women the protection of that sort of basic wardrobe—protection from ridicule, freedom to be themselves. It pains me physically to see a woman victimized, rendered pathetic, by fashion."

Section 1.6
Play Ball

War was not the only activity to change women's clothing. There were also sports. Women took up bicycling, tennis, swimming, skating, bowling, boxing, among other activities. All played a role in changing fashion.

Women did not participate nor were they allowed to watch the Ancient Greek Olympics, as the athletes were naked. However, the first official women's athletic competition occurred in the sixth century BC. The Heraean Games, dedicated to the goddess Hera (Zeus's wife), was for young, unmarried women. The participants were dressed in special tunics that cut just above the knee. Their right shoulder and breast were bared.

Women's tennis was incorporated into the modern Olympics in 1900. When tournaments resumed following World War I, Suzanne Lenglen, a French woman, stunned the world. She not only won, but she wore a one-piece cotton dress that revealed her forearms and was cut above the calf. She replaced her bonnet with a bandeau, a narrow band of ribbon or cloth.

While believing in style, she also firmly believed that clothes should not be restrictive. She turned professional in

1926. Her balletic playing style and brash personality made her revolutionary, nor was she above tossing her racket when she missed.

There is always one woman who stands out from the crowd. For swimming, it was Annette Kellerman, an Australian. She was the first woman to wear a one-piece bathing suit with a close fit. Before that time, swimming costumes, bathing dresses, or bathing gowns had high necks.

They were heavy and made of wool or flannel. They were accessorized with long black stockings. There were no bikinis or even tankini tops. Men generally swam nude or in their underwear.

What to wear to run a marathon depends on the weather. If it is cool, leggings are recommended. If it is hot, then shorts are just fine. This is true for men and women. Kathrine Switzer did not change the dress code; she changed the social environment when she officially ran the 1967 Boston Marathon.

While she had a number, an official attacked her to get her off the course. Staying ladylike and composed, she kept running. As Switzer said, "I'm going to finish this race on my hands and knees if I have to. Nobody is going to believe women deserve to be here if I don't finish this race." Marathons were no longer solely a male domain.

While we do not think of mountaineering as a sport, two books tell the story of women with a love for travel and adventure. In *Victorian Lady Travelers*, Dorothy Middleton wrote with great admiration for seven American and English women who went to remote corners of the globe to pursue their passion. As Victorians, they wore sensible clothes, but their skirts were long. In *On Top of the World*, Luree Miller demonstrated a love of travelers. She wrote of Americans and Englishwomen who were drawn to the secrets of Tibet.

When riding a bicycle, which became a fad in the 1880s, a split skirt was a necessity. It gave the illusion of wearing a long skirt. Panels helped to conceal the divide. When horseback riding, it enabled the rider to straddle a horse instead of riding sidesaddle.

In what other sport, did women have to look like women but play like men, but baseball? Women have played baseball since it became popular in the 1830s. In 1931, seventeen-year-old pitcher Jackie Mitchell, who was always a tomboy, signed a contract with a men's minor league team.

Soon after, she was in an exhibition game and played against the New York Yankees. In short order, she struck out both Babe Ruth and Lou Gehrig. There was lots of press. She went to her death claiming it was not staged, but her sinkerball.

In the 1930s and 1940s, amateur and semi-professional baseball uniforms for women consisted of satin shirts and long pants. With the advent of World War II, men entered the military, and women took over on the field. In 1943, the All-American Girl's Professional Baseball League was formed.

Players had to maintain a feminine image and follow strict guidelines, including always wearing skirts both on and off the field; wearing their hair a certain length; and complying with moral standards. The uniforms, modeled on skating and tennis, allowed the players to move. They had a short, flared, kicky hem disguising the athletic undershorts. Unfortunately, the skirts were so short that leg injuries often resulted when sliding into home. Baseball played by women was considered by some to be a novelty act.

Eventually, women were taken seriously as athletes.

Section 1.7
Amelia Earhart

At the beginning of her career, Amelia Earhart had to wear aviation suits that were designed for men and poorly fitted for a woman. There was nothing else available.

Having a sense of adventure at a young age, Amelia preferred practical women's clothing, such as pants, since she was a young girl. Women's clothing was not designed for 'active' women and often was not very utilitarian.

Some have called Amelia a 'tomboy' growing up. At the same time, she loved reading and spent hours in the family library.

Earhart did many things and earned many awards. She was a nurse during the 1918 Flu Epidemic. She gained flying experience, becoming the sixteenth woman to get her pilot's license, and she was an early supporter of the Equal Rights Amendment.

She was also one of the first aviators to promote commercial air travel, and she wrote best-selling books about her flying experience.

In 1920, she began saving money for flying lessons, cut her hair short like other female aviators (it was a bob), and purchased a leather jacket to wear when flying.

In 1928, Earhart became the first female passenger to cross the Atlantic by airplane, joining with pilot Wilmer Stultz. It brought her celebrity status.

In 1932, she made a non-stop transatlantic flight and was the first woman to do so. The United Press called her 'Queen of the Air'.

In 1933, Earhart created a clothing line for women. She had studied sewing as a young girl growing up. The clothing line was groundbreaking and eccentric. It consisted of practical clothes for 'active living'. It introduced blouses with longer shirttails that prevented the shirts from becoming easily untucked with every small movement. It was the first to build on separates.

Unfortunately, it was introduced during the depression when women did not have extra money for clothes. The line flopped.

In 1935, she was a visiting faculty member at Purdue University. She was an advisor, as well as a career counselor, to female students, the first in the country. She wanted to expand women's education beyond home economics. At the university, Earhart wore pants everywhere. This defied the school's rule that women were only allowed to wear skirts or dresses on campus.

When students complained to the Dean of Women, as they, too, wished to wear them, the dean always replied, "When you can fly an airplane solo across the Atlantic Ocean, then you can wear slacks in the Purdue dining hall."

That same year, Earhart became the first aviator to fly solo from Hawaii to California.

In 1937, attempting to fly around the globe, she was lost and presumably died. She was with her navigator, and they ran into bad weather.

In 1963, Earhart appeared on the eight cents postage stamp—wearing pants.

One of her quotes was: "Never do things others can do and will do if there are things others cannot do or will not do."

Section 1.8
Cowgirls and Bad Girls

The cowboy was 'born' in Mexico. Cowgirls were women homesteaders. Cowgirls personified the Western woman's can-do attitude and fascinated the United States, once the Homestead Act in 1862 was passed. The Act let women become landowners and, therefore, independent if, like anyone else, they had never borne arms against the government or aided or abetted an enemy of the United States.

The term 'cowgirl' first appeared in print in the early 1890s. It referred to a woman who tended free-range cattle. It also referred to women who identified with cowboy culture. Daughters of pioneer ranchers grew up alongside their brothers. They learned to ride and rope, as everyone's help was needed on the ranch.

Cowgirls traditionally wore a pair of gauntlets or protective gloves, a short skirt, tall lace-up boots, and often a red sash. They almost always wore a hat. It kept the sun out of their eyes, as well as rain, snow, dust, and whatever else that was blowing in the wind.

Stetson designed both the cowboy and cowgirl hats, but they didn't become part of the market of hats until 1885, but the first *official* cowboy hat, called 'Boss of the Plains' came in 1865. Its popularity didn't really come until the end of the nineteenth century. Instead, the preferred hat for a cowboy was the bowler hat. Not too many women wore bowlers.

Both hats were made with fur-felt and had the same function. However, the materials used to make each hat were slightly different: Cowgirl hats were made with synthetic fibers while cowboy hats were made with animal hair.

If there was a lack of familiarity with the cowboy hat rule, it was as follows: if you took someone's cowboy hat and put it on your head, then you were supposed to 'ride the cowboy', which meant have sex with them.

Lucille Mulhall (1851–1940) was often thought of as the first cowgirl. Teddy Roosevelt saw her do her thing, and he was only one of countless audiences that were introduced to the concept that a woman could rope and ride. She earned the nicknames 'Queen of the Saddle' and 'the Rodeo Queen'.

She performed in various Wild West shows and rodeos and formed her own troupe in 1913. Three years later, she went on to produce her own rodeo. She competed against men, able to break a bronco or lasso and brand a steer. It is not known if she ever rode the cowboy.

Tillie Baldwin (1888–1958) was one of America's most popular cowgirls. She was a rodeo contestant and performer in Wild West shows. She was one of the first women to attempt steer wrestling. She was inducted into the National Cowgirl Museum and Hall of Fame and the Rodeo Hall of Fame. She introduced a practical outfit when riding. It consisted of a middy blouse and bloomers with lots of room to move.

Belle Starr was a bad girl. She started life in a relatively well-off family, receiving a classical education and learning to play the piano. She became a gunslinger and outlaw, often referred to as 'the bandit queen'. She associated with other outlaws, such as Jesse James and the Younger brothers.

With one of her husbands, she was arrested for horse theft, and they both spent five months in jail. Upon their release, they resumed their criminal activities. She had become an expert shot and had learned fencing, rustling, bootlegging, thievery, and bribery over time.

Belle passed away just two days shy of her forty-first birthday, killed in an ambush. There were no witnesses, and no one was ever arrested.

Pearl Hart was also a bad girl and a stagecoach robber. She had cut her hair short and dressed in men's clothing. She was a novelty being a female stagecoach robber, causing a media frenzy. She became a popular feature of pulp western fiction.

Laura Bullion, another bad girl, was associated with Butch Cassidy and the Wild Bunch Gang in the 1890s. She was given the nickname 'Della Rose' by other members. After spending over three years in prison for a train robbery, she used different aliases and supported herself as a seamstress, a drapery maker, and an interior designer.

Section 1.9
Wild and Woolly West

What would stories about the Wild West be without poker? After all, Wild Bill Hickock died during a poker game while holding a pair of aces and a pair of eights.

Poker Alice or Alice Ivers Duffield Tubbs Huckert was born in England. She was raised in Virginia and sent to a boarding school, so she could become a refined young lady. She moved to Leadville in the Colorado Territory, married, and became enthralled with poker. She was very good!

When her husband died in a mining accident, she seriously began playing to meet her financial obligations, and she made a name for herself. She was drawing in large crowds. They liked to watch her play, and men were constantly challenging her. Saloon owners liked her as she refused to play poker on Sundays, keeping to her values. Alice was married twice more.

Over time, she also learned to play Faro and to deal. She moved from mining town to mining town, settling in Deadwood, South Dakota for a time. When she wasn't working, she went to other establishments to gamble. She prided herself on never cheating as that would have taken the fun out of the game.

Poker Alice was in much demand hired by saloons in Creede, Colorado, where gambling tables were set up in the streets, Leadville, and Buena Vista, Colorado, and Silver City, New Mexico. Her opening address was: "Praise the Lord and place your bets. I'll take your money with no regrets."

No, she did not wear pants. Instead, she spent her winnings, which could be substantial, on trips to New York to buy dresses and keep up with the latest fashions. She thought she could distract her opponents with her good looks. Even when she was in her fifties, she was considered to be attractive.

Poker Alice believed that her 'poker face' was one reason for her success. While most women of the time were expected to smile and show emotion, Alice would chomp on her cigar and show no emotion whatsoever. She also carried a gun, preferably a .38. She knew how to take care of herself.

Eleanor Dumont was another famous gambler, especially during the California Gold Rush. She had the appearance of a mustache on her upper lip, and she was also called a 'Madame Mustache'. She had her own gambling parlor, only letting in well-kept men and no women, except herself. She had a reputation for dealing fair.

The story goes that she was admired for her beauty and charm but kept men at a distance. While she flirted, it was to attract customers. Men came from all over to see the 'woman dealer' and her parlor was successful.

When gold dried up, she moved from place to place, gambling to build her reserves. In the 1860s, she opened a brothel. She committed suicide when she was about fifty after misjudging a play and losing a lot of money.

Annie Oakley, born Phoebe Ann Mosey, did not wear pants either, but she was a sharpshooter in Buffalo Bill's Wild West show. She trapped and hunted to take care of her impoverished family after their father died. She was only eight years old.

Later, she instructed women in marksmanship, believing strongly in self-defense and independence, as well as education although she herself did not attend school in early childhood.

Oakley also promoted the service of women in combat operations for the US armed forces. She wrote a letter to the President in 1898, "offering the government the services of a company of fifty 'lady sharpshooters' who would provide their own arms and ammunition should the United States go to war with Spain." Her offer was not accepted.

When Annie was fifteen years old, she won a shooting contest against Frank E. Butler, an experienced marksman. They later married and performed together in Buffalo Bill's Wild West show, Oakley shooting out a cigar from her husband's hand or splitting a playing card edge-on at thirty paces. In Europe, they performed before the Queen of Great Britain, the King of Italy, the President of France, and the Kaiser of Germany. She earned more than anyone except Buffalo Bill himself.

Section 1.10
Beards and Mustaches

There are several ways a woman can disguise herself as a man. Certainly, dressing as one is at the top of any list. So is assuming a man's walk and talk, including swearing or telling dirty jokes, hairstyle, short fingernails, and sitting with one's legs spread out rather than crossed. However, this section is about facial hair.

Beards never stop growing, even if you shave, wax, tweeze, or thread. As a note: tweezing is not painless. It can also cause scarring or pitting.

Having facial hair can change behavior and self-perception. Those with beards are often seen as angrier and more aggressive, as well as more masculine. Being clean-shaven is usually seen as a sign of being well-socialized and able to interact well with others.

Although just a sideshow, along with sword swallowers and extremely large or small people, the bearded lady at the circus has always attracted crowds.

Annie Jones was very well-known. She toured with P.T. Barnum when she was very young. Matthew Brady, the photographer, as well as other photographers, took her portrait. She died of tuberculosis when she was forty. She not only appeared as a sideshow attraction but also in dime museums.

Dime museums were low-brow institutions that were popular at the end of the nineteenth century in the United States. They were designed as centers for entertainment and moral education. Under the guise of education, they had attractions of human curiosities.

In France, Clémentine Delait rose to fame. Similar to Annie Jones, she was born in 1865 and presumably suffered from hirsutism, a female condition resulting in excessive growth of dark or coarse hair. It is most noticeable on the face. She had the condition from an early age, and she shaved regularly.

In 1900, while attending a carnival with a bearded lady, she claimed that she could grow a better beard. So she did. She began selling photographs and postcards of herself, toured Europe, and became something of a celebrity. She became even more popular when her husband died. She took good care of her beard, being very proud of it.

From 1840 until 1940, freakshows were at their height. Freakshows, also known as creep shows, featured human beings with a disability or those who were different in some way. They have been around for a long time. They were a common subject in Southern Gothic literature, including Carson McCuller's *The Heart is a Lonely Hunter*.

Today, one can look like one lived during the Roaring Twenties or ready to disco on the dance floor. There are so many different styles: Fu Manchus, Van Dykes, small beards, small mustaches, large mustaches, goatees, or some stubble. Fake beards can be made by hand from one hundred percent human hair. These are light and breathable. Transplanted beard hair can look completely natural.

Some movie stars are known for their facial hair, such as Sam Elliot, who often played ranchers or cowboys, and Tom Selleck. Selleck in *Magnum P.I.* is thought to have had the best mustache of all time. He has one in *Blue Bloods*.

Except for his sideburns, Elvis preferred to be clean-shaven. He had a beard for *Charro!* (1969). John Lennon had wild mutton-style sideburns in the late 1960s. Frank Zappa had a soul patch.

Burt Reynolds maintains that he got better roles, as well as women, when he had a mustache.

Anyone can acquire a beard and/or mustache. They are sold everywhere. Don't forget the mustache wax.

Section 1.11
Believe It or Not

Was there ever a woman Pope? Yes, if one counts Pope Joan in the ninth century during the Middle Ages. She supposedly reigned for two years. However, most scholars consider her to be a myth.

The story, nevertheless, is interesting. It spread throughout Europe in the thirteenth century, and it was believed for centuries. Joan had disguised herself as a man, a monk, and began religious training. She was a scholar and quickly rose in the church hierarchy before she became Pope John VIII. As Pope, she was able to hide her identity because of the robes she wore.

It was revealed that Pope Joan was a woman when she gave birth during a procession from St. Peter's. Some accounts state that she died during childbirth. Other accounts maintain that she was stoned to death by angry followers.

Processions held after this episode avoided this street, which had been called Via Sacra or the sacred way. The church removed her from its official lists. Again, per legend, a chair with a large hole was cut in a seat to check the sex of subsequent popes. A cardinal was responsible for checking.

Saint Wilgefortis reputedly lived in the fourteenth century. According to the legend, she was a teenager, a Portuguese noblewoman who was promised in marriage. To thwart the unwanted marriage, she took a vow of virginity and prayed that God would make her ugly. In response, she awoke from sleep to find that she had a beard. It was so repulsive the marriage was called off. Her disgraced and angry father had her crucified.

Prayer was very popular during the Middle Ages. Saint Wilgefortis was also very popular, particularly among people with severe problems. For women, this meant relief from abusive husbands.

Illuminated manuscripts and other art often showed the saint splayed on a cross, similar to Jesus Christ. A fiddler appears playing by her feet which are covered by a shroud. Her clothing is feminine and suggests softness.

A little closer to our time, if you can call the American Revolution closer, was Molly Pitcher. The stories about her are generally considered folklore, possibly a composite of more than one woman. Yet one woman, Mary Ludwig Hays, comes closest to Molly's description.

Mary followed her husband to war, where she performed mundane tasks, such as washing. This was not unusual. Molly was a popular nickname for Mary, and the buckets of water for washing were called pitchers. When her husband was wounded in battle, she took his place.

While on the battlefield, a cannon shot passed between her legs, taking away part of her petticoat. She was very brave. Unconcerned she went about her duties. She did not serve directly in battle again, but George Washington, upon hearing what had happened, promoted her. She became Sargent Molly, a title she used for the rest of her life.

According to legend, Betsy Ross made the first American flag in 1776, the one with red stripes and stars for each original colony arranged in a circle, when George Washington and two members of a secret committee visited her. But did she really? It would not be patriotic to say otherwise. Yes, she was plucky and practical, and she was a seamstress. In fact, she made flags.

However, almost a hundred years later, her grandson claimed the design was hers without any documentation. Betsy Ross might not have worn pants or defied society's expectations, but it is likely that she did not create the five-pointed star either.

Some legends stay with us for a very long time.

Section 1.12
Standing Tall and Strong

What woman today wants to be called an 'amazon'? The term carries a stigma, but it shouldn't.

In the Merriam-Webster dictionary, 'amazon' is defined as a tall, strong woman. In the *Encyclopedia of Amazons*, author Jessica Amanda Salmonson says, "In general terms, an amazon is any physically and/or intellectually powerful or superior woman. More specifically, any woman skilled at battle."

Of the stories told in Part 2, only two women have not been identified as an amazon in Salmonsons's list of 1,000 amazons. They are George Sand, a French author, and Billy Tipton, an American jazz musician.

In Greek mythology, the amazons were a race of strong and brave warlike women noted for their riding skills and pride. They lived at the outer limits of the known world. They were warriors and hunters who threw spears. They were also experts at ambush and charging when fighting.

They lived like soldiers and their purpose in life was to make war against men.

The amazons were a force with which to be reckoned.

So why have amazons been so disrespected? They wore pants. Their manner of dress and their weapons can be seen in art, such as pottery with black figures and on Greek friezes.

From the sixth century BC, they always wore armor and had a shield in battle. Their short tunic was fastened by a girdle. Their helmet was later replaced with a fur cap. They carried a bow and arrow, sometimes an axe.

Some believe that their armor had magical powers, but amazons were not invincible. Gunshots, as well as knives, could pierce their skin, just like anyone's.

The amazons appeared in various Greek myths.

One of the favorites is the queen Otera. She was the founder and later the first queen of the amazons. She was the consort of Ares and the mother of Hippolyta and Penthesilea.

Queen Penthesilea was perhaps one of the most famous, a warrior worthy of any of her Greek rivals. She and her followers helped Troy in the Trojan War. She confronted Achilles who killed her.

Queen Hippolyta's father was Ares, the war god. He gave her a golden, magical girdle or war belt that gave the wearer superhuman strength to show that she was superior to other amazons. Hercules, a Greek, was ordered by a king to steal the girdle for his ninth labor or task, causing a war between the amazons and the Athenians.

There are many versions of the myth. In one, Hercules takes the girdle by force. In another version, she gives it to him. In another version, Hercules was given the girdle as a ransom for the amazons whom he had taken captive when they had fought.

Queen Myrina, a noblewoman, won some battles, but lost others. She formed an alliance, after a peace treaty, with Egypt's ruler and conquered numerous cities, including those in Syria, and islands.

Thalestris was the last known amazon queen. She met Alexander the Great, bringing him three hundred women. She hoped to breed a race as strong and as intelligent as he. Many dispute this as a legend.

Did amazons really exist? They have certainly been the focus of research forever and ever. There are a number of ancient epic poems and legends that tell their stories, such as the *Iliad,* attributed to Homer. While there is no conclusion, more recent archaeological finds from the 1990s suggest that they did!

Section 1.13
Hail! Hail! Nuns and Queens

Monks and nuns performed many practical services in the Middle Ages, for they housed travelers, nursed the sick, and assisted the poor. Today, they do much of the same. The monastic life is not for everyone.

Their clothing has not changed much. One can almost always recognize a monk or a nun.

Marina was a woman masquerading as a monk. She probably lived in the fifth century, in a part of Lebanon. She was born to wealthy Christian parents. When her mother died when she was very young, her father raised her to be devoted. He intended to find her a suitable husband and then retire to a monastery.

When she realized this, she raised such a fuss that he took her with him. She dressed as a man, and they shared a cell and prayed together. Her soft voice was attributed to long periods of prayer. Some of her fellow monks thought she might be a eunuch.

When her father died, she continued to act as a male monk. With three others, she was sent to take care of the monastery business. They stayed at a lodge, where there was also a young soldier who seduced the beautiful innkeeper's daughter and instructed her to blame the young monk if she became pregnant. She did.

When informed, the abbot reprimanded Marina and told her to leave the monastery. She raised the baby but remained at the gates of the monastery as a beggar. After ten years, the monks convinced the abbot to allow Marina to return, which she did, but he then imposed on her hard labor.

Marina became ill when she was forty years old and died. During the ritual of cleaning her body and changing her clothes, her secret was discovered. The abbot and the innkeeper, as well as the soldier and innkeeper's daughter, were appalled at what they had inflicted on her and asked for forgiveness.

During the funeral prayers, a one-eyed monk is said to have had his eyesight restored after he had touched the body. She is thought of as an example of resilience and piety.

Marina is a saint, and she is venerated in the Catholic Church, the Eastern Orthodox Churches, and the Coptic Orthodox Church. Coptic Orthodox Christians claim that her body has not decomposed.

Near the end of her autobiography, Catalina de Erauso (1585–1650) relates an exchange with a cardinal who remarks: "Your only fault is that you are a Spaniard."

"With all due respect," she reports that she replied, "that is my only virtue."

Catalina, also called 'the Lieutenant Nun', escaped from a Spanish convent when she was fifteen years old by climbing over a wall, before taking her vows to become a nun, disguising herself as a boy. She was tired of the nuns beating her, and she wanted freedom to drink and fight. At some point, she cut off her hair and threw it away. She was amoral and happily so. She was not a nice person.

In Spain, in the 1600s, following the reign of Isabelle I and her husband Ferdinand, a decline began due to Spain's decentralized power, weak kings, and a focus on the American colonies. Society believed that status was related to leisure and work was undignified. De Erauso took advantage of all that was happening.

After escaping the convent, Erauso began the life of a fugitive. She knifed rivals and killed soldiers. It might not all be true, but her adventures were exciting. Her actions were accomplished with bravado and flamboyance.

Always dressed as a man, her physique was quite masculine which helped her disguise: she was a cabin boy on a ship and went to America. She became a soldier of fortune in South America. In the military, she marched, was promoted, and damaged property when things did not go her way.

When she was in trouble, she went to a church for sanctuary.

Returning to Europe, she confessed that she was a woman, a claim verified by old women. They also verified that she was a virgin. At thirty-five years old, she was declared a blessed individual, provided she devoted herself to God. The Pope gave her permission to continue to dress as a man although he reminded her of the commandment to not kill.

Toward the end of her life, Erauso settled in South America, presumably Veracruz in Mexico. She established a business as a muleteer, a person who transports goods on pack animals, such as mules.

Nuns and would-be nuns are people. They come in all shapes and sizes.

So do queens.

Eleanor of Aquitaine (1122–1204) insisted on taking part in the second crusade in 1147 as she was the feudal leader of the soldiers from her French duchy. Although married to Louis, the king and leader, she went as head of her duchy, not as queen. She recruited her royal ladies-in-waiting and non-noble landholders. The crusade achieved little, and the Europeans suffered a humiliating defeat. She was blamed for the failure. She became queen of England when she married King Henry II in 1154.

Queen Isabelle I (1474–1504) was tough and determined. During most of her reign, which ended in 1504 with her death, Castille was at war. She did not lead troops onto the battlefield, but she traveled with every campaign, plotting strategy and tactics.

Catherine the Great (1729–1796) reigned as empress of Russia from 1762, after overthrowing her husband Emperor Peter III. She was a champion for the arts and greatly expanded Russia's borders.

And then there was Christina, Queen of Sweden (1626–1689). Her father, the king, wanted a boy, but even at birth, Christina fooled everyone. Her father was thrilled stating, "She'll be clever." Per his instructions, she was educated as a royal male would have been. She was known for education and patronage of learning and the arts.

As a child, Christina's mannerisms could probably best be described as those of a tomboy. She was taught and enjoyed fencing, horse riding, and bear hunting, rather than more feminine hobbies. She also had masculine features. As an adult, Christina walked like a man, sat and rode like a man, and could eat and swear like the roughest soldier. She never lost her rebellious nature.

No one was happy when she announced that she had no intention to marry, particularly the nobility, but she was happy studying ten hours a day. She showed abnormal interest in male attire and other women.

Christina was coronated in 1650. She abdicated in 1654. She left Sweden traveling as a man. While the reason for her abdication is not known, it is surmised that she preferred Catholicism to Sweden's state religion of Lutheranism.

When she was older, she spent much time in Rome where she took to wearing dresses with such a low neckline that she was rebuked by the Pope. Otherwise, her style did not change: she preferred a man's jacket in black satin which reached her knees, a short black skirt, and a large bow. She died when she was sixty-two years old in 1689 after falling ill.

Section 1.14
Let Freedom Ring

Ellen Craft was born into slavery. Her mother, too, was a slave, but her father was their slaveholder, and she bore a strong resemblance to her father's other children, her siblings. She was separated from her mother when she was eleven years old when she was given as a wedding present to her half sister.

Ellen married when she was twenty. Her husband, too, was a slave who had been separated from his family. They did not have children when slaves as they didn't want their children to suffer the same fate as they had.

Both Ellen and her husband had privileges. With passes, they were allowed to travel locally.

Two years after marrying, her husband devised a plan for them to escape. She would wear a disguise as an invalid man and the master of her husband as they were aware that people would look strangely at a white woman traveling alone with a black man.

Most escapes took place under the cover of darkness. However, they traveled by day using Ellen's fair skin to hide in plain sight. She cut her hair short and wore a top hat and spectacles. She applied poultice to cover the fact that she lacked facial hair. She also had to make her own trousers.

They went from Georgia to Pennsylvania by steamboats and train and then proceeded to a black community in Massachusetts. If asked, they said that they were heading north to see a specialist. Neither could read nor write, so they bandaged Ellen's arm in order that she would not have to sign registration papers for travel or lodging. The plan worked although Ellen was once scolded for saying 'thank you' to her husband/man-servant.

Anna Maria Weems escaped from slavery with the help of members of the Underground Railroad. She disguised herself as a male carriage driver.

Anna Maria and her younger sister were separated from their family when Anna was seven years old. Her mother and two brothers were released from slavery while freedom for her sister was negotiated and paid for with the help of abolitionists in the United States and England. Anna Maria ran away from her slaveholder when she was fifteen years old.

The journey to Canada was very dangerous because of the Fugitive Slave Act of 1850, which mandated that if caught, slaves be returned to their owners, even if they were in a northern or free state. Her trip took over two months, of which she was in hiding and dressed as a young man known as Mr. Joe Wright, for six weeks.

As Mr. Joe Wright, Anna wore a driver's uniform, cap, and bow tie. She had been taught how to carry herself like a young man.

John and Arabella, her parents, had a daughter, Mary, who was born free. They were able to reunite with their other children. The family lived in Canada.

Mary Fields, also known as Stagecoach Mary and Black Mary, was born a slave. She stood six feet tall and weighed two hundred pounds. She was the first black woman employed as a postwoman in the United States. She worked near Cascade in Montana and the Montana territory.

She was emancipated by the Civil War and found work as a chambermaid on a steamboat. In 1895, when she was sixty years old, she got her job as a postal carrier using a stagecoach in bad weather, not unusual in Montana. She had a fearless demeanor and always carried many firearms.

She was much respected and beloved. When the town passed a law banning women in saloons, the mayor granted her an exemption. Volunteers rebuilt her home when it burned down. When she retired at seventy-one, she babysat for many children of Cascade.

When she died at the age of eight-two, the town had never seen such an attendance at a funeral.

Harriet Tubman was born into slavery. She is probably best known for her work with the Underground Railroad. Before the Civil War, she made thirteen missions to rescue about seventy slaves with a price on her head in the dark of night. She was a clever tactician, always taking precautions, with strong personal discipline.

During the Civil War, she served as an armed scout and spy for the Union Army after she was recruited. She was always at risk. She was the first woman to lead an armed assault.

After the war, she was an advocate for women's rights and suffrage. Despite the efforts of the slavers, Tubman and the fugitives she assisted were never captured. Years later, she told an audience: "I was a conductor of the Underground Railroad for eight years, and I can say what most conductors can't say—I never ran my train off the track, and I never lost a passenger."

Elizabeth Van Lew was the daughter of a wealthy couple in Richmond Virginia's high society. She was sent to a Quaker school in Philadelphia where it is believed she developed her anti-slavery sentiments. She often brought provisions and water to Union soldiers at a local prison, as well as passing messages to and from the prison.

She got a job for Mary Bowsers, as a dim-witted illiterate slave in the household of Jefferson Davis. She was anything but. Together Elizabeth and Mary built and operated a spy ring for the Union Army. They were intent on bringing down the Confederacy.

Section 1.15
British Babes

It was not only American women who were audacious and undertook courageous activities as men. Among British women, there were sailors and surgeons, pirates and paupers, and upper class and lower.

Mary Wolverston, also known as Lady Killigrew, who lived during the 1500s, was born to piracy. Her father was a pirate as was her husband, who was from an ancient Cornish family. This was at the beginning of the Golden Age of Piracy when Queen Elizabeth 1 ruled.

As long as piracy happened far away and in a manner that allowed the government deniability, there was no problem. This was especially so as Mary and her husband bribed officials with large fees. However, Lady Killigrew and her husband plundered in English waters, not the high seas, and English as well as foreign ships.

Mary was eventually arrested for fencing stolen goods. The queen pardoned her in later life.

A confusing and exaggerated biography of Mary Firth was published in 1662, three years after she had died. Her nickname was Moll (or Mal) Cutpurse, as she was a pickpocket and thief for the London underworld, and Moll was a nickname for Mary, a young woman of an untrustworthy character at the time. In public, she wore a doublet and baggy breeches, smoking a pipe.

Firth enjoyed the attention she drew. She liked making people uncomfortable. By the 1620s, she procured young women for men, as well as respectable male lovers for middle-class wives. Society did not approve.

After being caught, she escaped the gallows with a bribe. She died of dropsy or heart failure in London.

When she was twenty-five years old, Hannah Snell in the 1700s assumed the identity of her brother-in-law, James Gray, after her husband deserted her. She decided to follow him. No one knows why as he was a philanderer and he left her in debt. It is always possible that she was seeking money and adventure.

As a man, Snell joined the British Royal Marines and fought with them for four years. She was shot twelve times in the legs and once in the groin. Not wanting to reveal that she was a woman and lose her pension, she decided to live with the pain and removed the musket ball in the groin herself.

After receiving her pension, Snell retired and opened a pub named 'Female Warrior'. It did not succeed. She married twice and had children.

There are numerous accounts of her life. Not all of them are true.

On a more upscale note, there was Dr. James Barry. He was born Margaret Anne Bulkley in Ireland. Her early schooling was that of a young woman who would get married. Barry had taken the name of his uncle, an artist. He knew he had to start thinking like a man if his disguise was to work. He did what he always dreamed about and went to medical school, the best in Scotland, and then joined the British Army.

Barry had a reputation for being tactless, impatient, argumentative, and opinionated, but he was also considered to have had a good bedside manner. He was short with a slight build, unbroken voice, delicate features, and smooth skin.

Dr. Barry was the first female British surgeon. He was in the post for forty-six years, rising to the position of Inspector General of Hospitals. Wherever Barry served, improvements were made to sanitary conditions and the diet of both the common soldier and other under-represented groups.

Barry's disguise was discovered at his death. Although he repeatedly expressed the preference that his body not be examined, his preference was ignored or not known. Upon the discovery of his sex, the British Army was embarrassed and covered it up.

Section 1.16
Plundering Pirates

Blackbeard, whose treasure was never found, might be the most feared pirate of all time. William Kidd was the oldest active pirate during the Golden Age of Piracy.

While he worked the seas until he retired when he was fifty-four years old, most pirates did not live more than five years after becoming one. Mary Reid and Anne Bonny were legendary female pirates. Sayyida al-Hurra of Northern Morocco was known for her piracy against Spain and Portugal. Zheng Yi Sao, better known as Ching Shih, ruled the South China Sea.

Although very few women become pirates, these are some of the most brazen.

Prior to the 1970s, China's sovereignty over the South China Sea islands had never been challenged by any external forces, and today China claims about 80% of the area.

Back in the Qing dynasty (1644–1911) in the early days of the nineteenth century, Ching Shih (1775–1844) lived and pillaged. She was the mastermind behind a floating criminal empire. From a poor family, she started working in a brothel as a prostitute. Then she married a pirate. He had been brash and loud, she was quiet and calculating with a business mind. By 1806, every seagoing vessel in the region paid tribute to them for protection.

With her husband's death, she married again, a man named Chang Pao, and she made him head of her huge fleet. This was a good move as he was respected and her fleet was unstoppable.

Her fleet consisted of at least 40,000 pirates, with some estimates ranging as high as 80,000. In terms of power, she was unprecedented and unstoppable. She was not afraid of the Chinese Imperial Navy. She helped negotiate a truce among the leaders of the pirate fleets into one confederation. Six fleets, each flying a colored flag—red, black, blue, white, yellow, and purple—would essentially operate as a pirate navy. Hers was red.

The red flag flown by naval vessels in wartime meant a fight to the finish. Among pirates, flying a red flag signaled 'no quarter' to any ship's crew that resisted. It guaranteed the safety of all aboard if the ship surrendered without a fight.

Ching Shih's fleet consisted of large vessels that could carry up to 800 tons of cargo and as many as 40 cannons. Junks were excellent ocean-going sailing ships with a flat bottom and a very high stern; their rudder could be raised which allowed them to enter shallow waters when other large ships could not. At its peak, about 1809, the Pirate Confederation totaled some 1,800 junks. It terrorized the Chinese coast and threatened naval superpowers.

In 1808, the Chinese Qing government was overwhelmed in the South China Sea. It decided it was time to do something about the pirates, as they were disrupting commerce. The government gathered a massive fleet of warships and set a trap for them.

Ching Shih realized that government harassment would never end. She used her considerable power to negotiate a pardon for herself and her sailor. She also received a cash settlement and a title of nobility and was even allowed to keep a small flotilla of ships and sailors. In 1810, it was the end of the Pirate Confederation.

Ching Shih actually retired. Most sources say that she spent her last years running a brothel and gambling den. She died at sixty-nine years old, wealthy and respected.

Over a century later, Huang Bamei (1906–1982), also a Chinese pirate, plundered, kidnapped, and murdered traders and even ordinary people. She earned the nickname 'Two Guns' because of her use of two guns in battle if necessary. She lied to avoid capture. She participated in the Sino-Japanese War and the Chinese Civil War. In later life, she eventually relocated to Taiwan where she died. Her body was moved to the mainland.

Although very few women became pirates, Grace O'Malley was a pirate and trader through family connections that controlled the Western coast of Ireland. This redhead cut her hair short. In control in the 1560s, she plundered and raided English and Spanish shipping vessels. Her exploits are well-remembered, but she spent eighteen months in prison.

Upon her release, O'Malley resumed her piracy. When she was sixty-three years old, the British impounded her fleet. With nowhere else to turn, she appealed to Queen Elizabeth I. She depicted herself as a tired and broken old woman and asked for a small amount for maintenance for the time she had left. She also asked the queen to return her ships and release one of her captured sons. Her plea was successful, but she didn't keep her promise and continued her activities until her death in 1603.

She passed away when she was over seventy years old, which was a long life for a pirate.

Rachel Wall holds the possible distinction of being the first American female pirate.

Born in 1760 to a devout family, she was very unhappy and spent her free time at a nearby waterfront. Rescued by a man named Wall, whom she later married, he led her into piracy. Following a storm, he stood on the deck of their ship and yelled for help. When help arrived, the 'good people' were murdered and their goods stolen.

When Wall's husband died accidentally and washed out to sea, she continued sneaking onto boats and stealing whatever she found.

In 1789, she was found guilty of stealing a bonnet, shoes, and buckles from a young woman walking along the road. This was highway robbery. She denied the events, but she was found guilty.

Section 1.17
And Justice for All

This is not a treatise on LGBTQ rights. This section is here to show how difficult it was for women and others to dress with comfort and ease, as they pleased. It is not a straightforward story and many countries and dates have not been included.

In the beginning, it started with the Bible, not Genesis, but Deuteronomy. The text of 22.5 states: "A woman shall not wear a man's garment, nor shall a man put on a woman's cloak, for whoever does these things is an abomination to the LORD your God." According to the Law of Moses, cross-dressing was clearly something that one did not do.

There has been much discussion as to what this passage means. Is it about modesty? The New Testament does not specifically address the clothing of men and women other than a call to modesty. Some scholars believe that cross-dressing was associated with homosexuality. Some conservatives have taken this passage to mean a woman cannot wear pants or slacks.

In early Rome, both pants and boots were banned. As the code read: no one shall wear pants or boots. If any man after the issuance of this regulation of Our Clemency should obstinately persist in such costumes, he shall be punished. At issue was confusion between civilians and those in the military.

By the fifth and sixth centuries, suddenly the so-called barbarian custom of trousers with a sleeved top had become the official uniform of the Roman court. If you were close to the emperor, that's what you wore.

The toga was a symbol of social control and punishment. Only male citizens of Rome were allowed to wear them. A toga was s large piece of cloth, almost always wool, usually white, and expensive, that was about eighteen feet long and six feet wide. It was draped across the shoulders and around the body. Slaves were needed to get dressed.

It was worn over a much more practical plain white linen tunic. Prostitutes wore the toga to distinguish themselves from other women and attract customers more easily. Adulteresses, like others who exhibited licentious behavior, were forced to wear a toga. Prostitutes and adulteress strove for the sexual freedom of men.

Following the French Revolution in 1789, Paris established a law, which only allowed women's pants if urban authorities approved of it. Officials believed that this effectively kept women in their place. The law was modified in 1892 and 1909 to allow women to wear trousers if they were "holding a bicycle's handlebar or the reins of a horse." It was assumed that they were riding.

Many societies prohibited women from performing on stage, so boys and men took the feminine role. In the sixteenth century, cross-dressing was normal practice in the theater. It was a gradual process that women started playing women. By 1901, it was no surprise to see women on stage.

Both sexes wore clothes made of wool, but they varied in quality. Wool could be fine and expensive or coarse and cheap. The rich wore fine-quality wool. The poor wore coarse wool. However, only the rich could afford cotton and silk.

In the mid-fourteenth century, laws lay down which materials the different classes could wear, to stop the middle classes from dressing 'above themselves'. However, most people ignored the law and wore what they wanted and could afford.

It didn't get any better as time went by.

Harrods in London prohibited female customers in trousers from entering its store until 1970.

International luxury hotels, for instance, still had bans on women wearing trousers during the 1970s.

In the nineteenth and twentieth centuries, some US cities passed legislation barring women from wearing trousers. Among these US cities was San Francisco in 1863 that prohibited "dress not belonging to his or her sex." This law was in effect until 1974. Another city is Columbus, Ohio, which passed a similar law in 1848.

It was the first. Other cities included Chicago in 1851, Houston in 1864, and Orlando in 1907. These laws were often part of anti-vice campaigns, targeting vagrancy, indecency, public drunkenness, and nudity.

The Anti-Masquerading Ordinance of 1898 that dictated that one could not conceal one's face in public was enacted in Los Angeles' in an attempt to intimidate the growing queer subculture. Laws varied greatly between jurisdictions. New York State enacted a bill in 1845 to provide for public safety. Such laws have been challenged as a violation of the First Amendment.

By the beginning of the twentieth century, gender inappropriateness was increasingly considered a sickness and public offense.

Police used these laws and attitudes to become increasingly aggressive against the gay community. In 1969, a riot against the police at the Stonewall Inn, a gay bar in Greenwich Village, for harassment began to change attitudes. Following the riot, arrests decreased and the majority of anti-cross-dressing laws have been overturned.

Change happens.

In 1923, the US Attorney General declared that it was legal for women to wear trousers anywhere.

Until 1993, it was the unofficial rule on the floor of the US Senate that women weren't supposed to wear pants. Later in 1993 two women senators did just that. Female support staff followed soon after. The rule was amended later that year by Senate Sergeant-at-Arms Martha Pope to allow women to wear trousers on the floor.

Time progresses and fashion evolves, so it is increasingly difficult to even define what 'cross-dressing' entails from a law-enforcement perspective.

Section 1.18
The More Things Change...

Education in the United States has certainly changed.

Since colonial times, colleges had been for men, reserved for the sons of the Eastern elite. In early America, girls were taught reading usually by their mother to promote religious instruction. They did not learn writing.

Oberlin College in Ohio, opening in 1833, was the first higher learning institution to admit women in the United States. It went coed in 1837. Three of the four women who started at the time graduated with a Bachelor of Arts.

Cornell University was the only Ivy League school to admit women from its founding in 1865.

It was not until the 1960s that other Ivies began accepting women. Princeton and Yale began admitting women in 1969, and Brown followed in 1971. Dartmouth held out until 1972. After that, only a single Ivy League school maintained its men-only admission policy: Columbia University was the last holdout, finally opening its doors to women in 1983.

With more women than men enrolled in college, it is now harder for women to get in.

Movies have changed little. They still aim to entertain and enthrall, no matter who is directing.

Dorothy Arzner (1897–1979) was the first woman to join the Directors Guild of America and the first woman to direct a sound film. She worked during Hollywood's Golden Age (1926–1959) when movies such as *Wizard of Oz* and *Ben-Hur* were made. She directed Clara Bow in her first talkie and Fredric March in his first leading role.

Azner was a trailblazer. She not only had a long career, but she had a forty-year relationship with a woman, a dancer and choreographer, who was sixteen years older than her. She never hid her sexual orientation. She cut her hair short, and her unconventional clothes were suits and straight dresses.

Disney made Mulan twice, once in 1998 as an animated musical and the second time in 2020 as live action. The second time was based on the original. The original was based on Chinese folklore.

In the movie, Mulan dresses as a man after cutting her hair to take her father's place in the army as he has no chance of survival. She flees with his armor, horse, and sword.

Kathryn Bigelow became the first woman to win an Academy Award for best director, for her movie *The Hurt Locker* (2008). To date, she is the only woman to do so.

Ava DuVernay has also had a successful career in Hollywood, but it has been a long time coming. She was the first African-American woman nominated for a Golden Globe for Best Director and the Academy Award for Best Picture for *Selma* (2014).

There are few women directors today, except for Sophia Coppola, Greta Gerwig, and Gina Prince-Bythewood. The later directed *The Woman King* (2022). Both she and star Viola Davis received glowing acclaim for the historical action drama.

In the seventies, everyone wore pants. There were simple and comfortable pants for both days and evenings for women. One could wear their blue jeans with bell bottoms or not. Traditionalism was out. Hot pants came out in 1970, but not everyone could wear them.

In 1971, pants were first allowed as part of the uniform of dental hygienists, allowing hygienists to sit while working on patients.

Does anyone remember getting dressed up to fly? Now anything goes. Athletic wear is now the clothing of choice, but that does not mean sloppy. Still, many just look sloppy.

In 2021, Aspercreme introduced a commercial called 'Warriors'. It featured two women, both with swords and wearing boots, fighting each other. One wore a breastplate underneath a long red robe. The other had on a leather breastplate and a short skirt. It was supposedly reminiscent of ancient Rome.

However, in ancient Rome, female gladiators only wore loincloths, so the audience could clearly see that they were women. As for the weapons, such as shields, their equipment was the same as for the male gladiators.

Some historians claim that this partial nudity was not meant to be erotic and that it was simply the most practical way for warriors to dress. However, as the vast majority of the audience members were men, it's extremely possible that at least a few of these men were excited by more than just the fighting.

Many free, upper-class men decided to become gladiators because they wanted fame, glory, and the chance to win prize money that could make them rich. Women were no exception. In fact, the vast majority of female gladiators took the job of their own free will, despite being seen as a threat to women's role in society.

the more they stay the same.

Introduction to Part 2

In this section of the book, the stories of ten-plus women are told. This includes their background, their circumstances, and their physical characteristics if known.

Hatshepsut, the pharaoh queen, aspired to hold on to her power. Joan of Arc simply wanted protection. Female pirates Mary Read and Anne Bonny would do whatever was asked of them.

During wars, women wanted to show their patriotism, so they enlisted as men. Calamity Jane sometimes wore man's clothing, and sometimes she didn't. Everyone agreed that she was very generous and warm-hearted.

Despite the differences, in terms of personality and the times in which they lived, there are similarities.

Several women, such as Calamity Jane and George Sand, as well as Deborah Sampson and Catalina de Erauso, wrote their autobiographies. However, Calamity Jane's 'book' was more of a pamphlet, which she wrote for publicity. Amelia Earhart wrote several books.

Both Calamity Jane and Belle Starr, as well as other cowgirls, knew how to shoot. So did Annie Oakley and Mary Fields. The last three are described in Part I.

Marie Curie and Florence Nightingale had careers in medicine, both are included in Part I.

Some jobs simply could not be done in a long skirt. Charley Parkhurst, for example, was a stagecoach driver. Billy Tipton wanted to travel with a band and play jazz. And no one told George Sand what to do.

Section 2.1
Hatshepsut

Hatshepsut was one of the few female pharaohs of Ancient Egypt. According to various Egyptologists, she is "the first great woman in history of whom we are informed." She is considered one of Egypt's great pharaohs, be they male or female.

Dates are very difficult when it comes to Ancient Egypt. As an example, after Hatshepsut's death, an attempt was made to remove her from official accounts, despite her many accomplishments. This was done by destroying her statues and defacing her monuments.

There were other female pharaohs, including Cleopatra and possibly Nefertiti who might have ruled briefly after her husband's death, as well as several lesser-known women.

Hatshepsut was the fifth Pharaoh of the Eighteenth Dynasty, ruling from about 1478 BC until her death, almost twenty-two years later. In Ancient Egypt, patriarchal bloodlines were revered. She was the daughter of Pharaoh Thutmose I and his principal wife. Upon his death and that of her half brother, Thutmose II, whom she had married, she ruled as regent to her stepson/nephew, Thutmose III. Since he was only two years old, she had a lot of power, even as a coruler. Several years later, she assumed the position of pharaoh, a divine office.

As pharaoh, she undertook the royal naming convention, symbolizing worldly power and holy might. The five names in the convention linked the pharaoh to the people and the gods. Her personal name was the one given at birth.

The throne name was the first of two names written inside a cartouche. A cartouche had an oval border, indicating that the five names, if written in hieroglyphics, were to protect the bearer from evil spirits in life and after death. It symbolized the pharaoh's status as ruler of all that the sun encircled.

Hatshepsut knew what she had to do as a woman in a patriarchal society to keep her position. She was a regent for a young boy who was not her son. Previously only mothers were allowed to rule on behalf of their sons. And then she became king. She asserted that she was her father's choice as pharaoh. In the statues she constructed of herself, she was ambiguous and androgynous, creating a masculine version to establish herself as part of the establishment.

When she first showed herself as sovereign, she wore a tight-fitting dress. It showed off her hips and thighs. Later, she created statues that made her more masculine with buff biceps and muscles, a wide chest, strong legs, a square jaw, and a masculine face.

Hatshepsut used her regency to create her kingship. She built extensive temples to celebrate her reign, so the public became used to seeing a woman in a powerful role. It can be argued that she placed in power men, or the Egyptian elite, who could further advance their own wealth. They were confident that she could handle Egyptian wealth and trade. It helped that she had a record of success in different fields, such as that of High Priestess, and that she had come to power at a time of peace and prosperity which continued during her reign.

In other words, she took on traditionally male roles and was depicted as a male pharaoh, with traditionally male garb, including a false beard. Hatshepsut brought artistry to her land. She sponsored one of Egypt's most successful trading expeditions, bringing back gold, ebony, and incense from Africa.

Priests were important, too, and she emphasized her piety. They told a story about her divine birth, involving the gods Amun and Ahmose. According to the oracle of Amun, it was proclaimed that Hatshepsut be the pharaoh. She strengthened this proclamation by carving more proclamations on her monuments.

Hatshepsut had long hair of a golden color and red-painted fingernails. She was powerful with an iron will.

Her stepson, Thutmose III, was very jealous of his aunt, even though she was a queen. He called her a cross-dresser. No one cared.

When Hatshepsut was no longer in the picture, Thutmose III became pharaoh on his own. Officially, he ruled for fifty-four years, beginning when he was two years old with Hatshepsut his co-regent. Historians consider him to have been a military genius, conducting seventeen campaigns in twenty years. He expanded Egypt's border as never before. He was also a great builder, constructing over fifty temples and commissioning the building of tombs for nobles with great craftsmanship.

As a person, he was also an accomplished horseman, archer, and athlete. Except for his personal issues with Hatshepsut, he was considered to be sincere and fair.

Ancient Egyptians walked like anyone else. There is nothing that suggests otherwise, except the 1987 song *Walk Like an Egyptian* sung by the Bangles. Tomb paintings created a pleasant afterlife for the dead. Their heads, when buried, were placed facing the rising sun, a popular god, so that they could greet the day.

Egyptians thought of their rulers as young with fit bodies, and so it was in their art. Men are shown with broad shoulders, slim bodies, and muscular arms and legs. Women are shown with small waists and flat stomachs. The left leg usually led because the heart is on the left side. The heart was not only the center of emotion but also intelligence and will.

Scenes were drawn with a two-dimensional perspective. Men were usually in red while women, who did not work outside, had a yellowish tone. Royalty was depicted with self-confidence. The elite are in their best dress. Egyptian art is always immediately recognizable.

Cleanliness and personal appearance were very important to Ancient Egyptians, regardless of station. Poorly groomed people were considered inferior. The wealthiest would hire a barber to live with them and clean-shave them every day. In addition to hygiene, vanity, and simplicity were motivations for being clean-shaven. The masses could not afford a full-time barber, so they turned to the service of the humble street barber.

High Priests opted for full-body shaves. Initially, tweezers were used to pull hair. There was also waxing and sugaring. Over time, blades and razors were produced, which made life a whole lot easier for Ancient Egyptians, as well as barbers. Kings were often buried with jewel-encrusted or solid gold razors, ensuring a smooth look in the afterlife.

Women wore their hair long under a wig while men cut their hair short or shaved their head. There were two styles of wigs: a short wig with bangs made of small curls that overlapped one another. The bangs were short enough to show some forehead, while the side and back covered the ears and neck. The alternative was a bulky wig with curls of hair covering both shoulders.

Most wigs were deep black. Blonde wigs, less popular, were also impressive.

The most expensive wigs looked like real hair. Wigs had a few purposes. In addition to being decorative: they signaled rank, helped protect shaven scalps, helped maintain hygiene from head lice, and hid gray or white hair. Henna helped, but wigs were better. Egyptians believed that wigs were necessary in the afterlife as they wanted to appear wealthy with beautiful hair.

Both men and women wore jewelry and used make-up. Most noticeable was heavy eyeliner along the lower and upper eyelid. It was usually made of black kohl, a common lead ore that came from a mineral. Egyptians not only thought it looked beautiful but also believed it was protection from dirt and dust and the harsh rays of the sun.

Only lower classes got tattoos, but everyone painted their hands with henna. Henna was a firmly established tradition as it was safe, temporary, and painless. Originally, henna was associated with pharaohs and then women.

While commoners were not allowed to wear headdresses or hats, thick head hair in the early days was a status symbol. Wigs were always popular, as were hair extensions for both men and women in the upper levels of society, such as pharaohs and queens. Henna helped, but wigs were better.

The beard was a divine attribute of the gods. A pharaoh showed his status as a living god with a false beard. It looked more like a goatee than a beard. False beards were worn during the pharaoh's life as well as in his death. This is one of the oldest customs of Ancient Egypt. It was held in place by a ribbon tied over the head and attached to a gold chin strap. It was made of stone and metal and was passed on from generation to generation.

A false beard was also present on the pharaoh's sarcophagus. When a pharaoh died, the beard was represented as the god Osiris himself to facilitate the journey in the world of souls.

There were several types of false beards. The rectangular one was the most common, and it was worn by most pharaohs. The curved one was most often worn by the gods. It could also be integrated into a mask, such as the mask of Tutankhamun. The headdress was worn by a god or pharaoh.

It symbolized their importance and separated them from everyone else. It was usually called a nemes. It was made of stiff linen and very colorful. This stiff linen headdress covered the head with flaps that hung down the sides and over the shoulders.

Most people went barefoot, including royal officials. Sandals often identify a person's social status. Eventually, they became associated with pharaohs and the wealthy.

Both men and women wore an amulet for protection or to ensure well-being. An amulet could be a necklace, ring, or bracelet. It might be made of ceramic, stone, metal, bone, or gold. It was a piece of jewelry that was believed to have special power through magic or blessing that kept away disease and evil. Amulets were used by both living Egyptians and their deceased brethren. It was both decorative and practical.

On the deceased, amulets were usually worn or placed to transfer their powers directly to the owner. Two-fingered amulets were exclusively for the dead. These amulets were found on the lower left of the torso where an incision was made during mummification when the internal organs were removed. They were meant to heal the wound and protect the person in the afterlife.

No one wore pants in Ancient Egypt. It was too hot. Most clothing was made out of white linen, as it kept the wearer cool. Status was always important. The higher the status, the thinner the material.

Women usually wore full-length dresses that would either have one or two shoulder straps but minimal sewing. The material was always very simple. Upper-class women wore fine dresses with shoulder straps and a shawl or a cape or robe. Women tended to wear more jewelry than men, especially across the chest.

Men wore wraparound skirts belted at the waist. This style of dress was consistent across class, but higher class Egyptians wore more finely crafted pieces.

Lower classes wore much simpler garments made of less expensive cloth.

Pharaohs wore a half-pleated kilt wound around the body with a pleated section drawn to the front. Pharaohs also wore, as symbols of power, leopard or lion skins over their shoulders and a lion's tail hanging from their belt. On their heads, they wore the nemes while the nobility wore the khat or head cloth.

Even Hatshepsut wore a false beard. During her reign, she had done a lot: secured and expanded borders; enriched elites; built houses of stone for the gods; and, engaged in risky trade ventures. All told she left the country better off than she had found it.

Section 2.2
Joan of Arc

Joan of Arc was born in 1412 or 1413 and baptized. She was a peasant in a remote part of France, the dominant kingdom in Western Europe. With her family, she was forced to flee at least once when her village was sacked. She was illiterate, similar to less than twenty percent of the population at the time. In most places, literacy did not experience significant increases until the Enlightenment and industrialization.

She was born during the Hundred Years' War (1337–1453), a significant conflict in the later Middle Ages, between the French and the English over claims to the French throne. Over time, it grew into a wide-ranging power struggle, and it had a long-lasting effect on European history. While there were several truces, they didn't last.

The outbreak of war was motivated by a gradual rise in tension between the kings of France and England over territory. English monarchs had historically held titles and lands within France. This made them vassals, people who received protection and land from a lord or monarch in return for loyalty and service. It was fueled by rising nationalism. It virtually destroyed the feudal nobility and thereby brought about a new social order.

The war brought much suffering. Life was harsh, with a limited diet and little comfort. Peasants worked hard every day except Sundays and holy days in the blazing sun, rain, or snow. Most peasants with their family lived in tiny one- or two-room thatched cottages. The environment was unhygienic and disease-ridden. The water supply left much to be desired.

The war finally ended in 1453, twenty-two years after Joan's death, when the French won. Like any other war, the people were traumatized and poorer although there was a shift in power to the people.

Joan's childhood was not remarkable although the family was somewhat better off than their neighbors. Like other female children, she made herself useful with housework, learning how to sew and spin wool, becoming adept at both. She had three brothers and a sister, with whom she looked after the family's animals. Her religious education was provided by the village priest, as well as through paintings, statues, and church windows.

Her mother's responsibility was to raise the children as good Christians. She taught Joan simple prayers. Joan was known for her piety and charity. Her father was a farmer, as was his father. He developed Joan's leadership abilities by serving in local government, creating a strain on their relationship. He had a certain respect within the community.

Women were subordinate to men, regardless of class, and were expected to ensure the smooth running of the household. Children had a 50% survival rate beyond age one and began to contribute to family life around age twelve.

Joan first heard a voice when she was thirteen years old when running in the fields with her friends. She did not say anything. The first of these voices spoke to her from her father's garden and was accompanied by a blinding white light. Over time, voices and visions came to her several times a day. The voices and visions told her that she was to free her country from the English and help Charles gain the French throne.

From the earliest times, rape was feared. Along with arson, treason, and murder, it was considered a capital offense, and rapists were subjected to a wide range of punishments, many of them quite brutal. Avoiding rape was a good reason, from a modern perspective, for a woman to dress as a man. Coupling that idea with the difficulty of travel at the time, it is easily understood why Joan of Arc put on men's clothing.

Any journey could be dangerous. Bandits, often soldiers who had no trade, lined the roads. In what would now take six hours by car took Joan eleven days to go from near her family home in Domrémy to the Château de Chinon, where she met with the future King of France. At that time, she began wearing men's clothing for protection. She told the King-to-be that she was sent by God to drive the English from France, and she asked for an army. She never showed any fear.

Charles sent Joan, who was about seventeen years old, to the siege of Orléans as part of a relief army.

Joan of Arc, furnished by the future king with a small army, entered the besieged city of Orléans in 1429. She believed that the men's clothing she wore and her short hair would avoid recognition when necessary for both protection and to expel the English from France and have Charles coronated as king. A French attack distracted the English troops, and Joan entered the city unopposed, bringing hope to the demoralized army, as well as needed supplies. Of special note was the loyalty given to her by her soldiers and the citizens.

Nine days later the siege was lifted. After that, Joan was called The Maid of Orléans.

During the fifteenth century, plate armor became the dominant form of protection for soldiers on the battlefield, and by about 1500, it had all but displaced mail and fabric armor or relegated them to secondary functions such as protecting the joints and other easily exposed areas.

Joan was ready for battle. Now her sword was called the Joan of Arc Sword or sometimes the sword of Saint Catherine. It was a typical medieval arming sword or side-arm. It had five crosses engraved in the center of the blade. This was not unusual, but it differentiated the sword from others. There is otherwise little known about her sword.

Although not at the front line, Joan was wounded when an arrow pierced her armor at the shoulder. After dressing her wound, she returned to the battlefield.

Joan preferred her banner to her sword because it was a real morale booster, once declaring that with her banner she wouldn't have to kill anyone. Often she took off her helmet so the soldiers could see her, encouraging them with her cry of 'Go boldly'. King Charles gave each of Joan of Arc's brothers a banner. It featured a blue shield, a sword, and two fleurs-de-lys. While Joan had permission to use this design, she preferred her own.

Joan took the king-to-be through an enemy country to be crowned. At his coronation, Joan in armor stood next to him with her banner.

Banners were used in wars to help soldiers identify friends or enemies. In the later years, medieval flags were almost exclusively emblazoned with a coat of arms or crest. This practice, called heraldry, had begun in the twelfth century. Each knight had his own flag or banner that identified him on and off the battlefield.

Banners were made of silk, possibly as fringe, and linen. They had to be sturdy and sensible. Joan's banner came to her in a vision. The background, looked like a white field, filled with white lilies. They were actually Fleur-de-lis. The world was depicted in the center as if it were being judged by Heaven. There were two angels on either side of the banner. Joan stitched the names Jesus and Maria on the side.

With the success of Orleans and the coronation of King Charles VII, Joan was expected to break the siege on Paris in 1429. She didn't, despite her great tactical skills. The city was defended by about 3,000 English and their allies. Joan was wounded with a crossbow bolt in the thigh. She was dragged from battle and ordered to withdraw. The king sounded the retreat.

In 1430, Joan of Arc was captured by the English and their French allies. She had been thrown from her horse and left outside the town's gates as they closed. She was held for over a year in a small, dark room with a small narrow window in a tower before her trial. She was chained to the wall during the day.

At night, shackles were attached to her ankles and then to a wooden block. She could not walk without assistance, nor sleep comfortably. She felt the male guards were going to attack at any time, so she was permitted to keep the laces and fastenings from her male garb.

At her trial, which began in January 1431, she was accused of heresy, witchcraft, and dressing as a man. There were other charges, many related, including acting upon visions that were demonic and refusing to submit her words and deeds to the church because she claimed she would be judged by God alone. She stated that it was her own choice to wear men's clothes and that she did so not at the request of men but by the command of God and his angels.

Joan was put on trial at the behest of bishops and theologians from English and related cities that she had recently attacked. They never intended to show mercy, as she was seen as both military and religious threats. The English came to view Joan as a witch.

Heresy was a capital crime. A heretic in Christianity is someone who has an opinion that is opposite to or against the official or popular opinion.

In the fourteenth century, burning at the stake became the most common method of putting to death those accused of witchcraft or heresy.

The trial called for a preliminary investigation into the life of the accused or Joan's character and habits. There was an examination of Joan's claims that she was a virgin. Nothing was found against her to support any of the charges. At the beginning of the trial, there were seventy charges against her such as attacking Paris on a religious holiday, throwing herself from a tower, and continuing to wear male clothes. These charges were put into twelve articles. Her wearing of men's clothing was the topic of five of the articles of accusations against her.

Throughout the proceedings, Joan showed remarkable composure. She did not want or like the spotlight, but she was convinced that she was called to a difficult task.

Charles VII, still unconvinced of Joan's divine mission or not wanting his newly returned crown to be taken away, made no attempt to rescue her.

Until much later, Joan did not perform any miracles. Most of the evidence of her religious character came from the trial.

Concerning cross-dressing, the medieval church's doctrine combined a general prohibition with an exception in cases of necessity, but it was not clear. Deuteronomy 22:5 was often quoted. In Joan's time, cross-dressing was a way for French women to join the cause against England.

There were also female saints, such as Saints Margaret and Thecla, who out of necessity, so they thought, wore men's clothes.

St. Margaret, one of Joan's voices, feared the loss of her virginity on her wedding night. She cut off her hair, put on men's clothing, left her husband, and joined a monastery.

St. Thecla followed her fiancé. She dressed as a man while with him and his advisors.

It was a common medieval archetype from the fifth to seventh centuries.

Joan felt comfortable and safe in such clothing although it was a sign of her heresy.

At trial, she said that she did so not at the request of men but by the command of God and his angels. She did not believe that wearing men's clothing was against the church.

At her trial, she was accused of wearing breeches, a mantle, a coat of mail, a doublet, a hose joined to the doublet with twenty laces, tight boots, spurs, a breastplate, buskins, a sword, a dagger, and a lance. She was also described as wearing furs, a coat over her armor, and sumptuous riding habits made of precious cloth.

Joan strongly believed her male clothes and haircut were appropriate for her calling, as she was a warrior and men's clothes were more practical. As well as being more practical, they also allowed her to transcend the limits of her own sex and participate in battles as the military leader and protector of France. It was crucial to uphold this image among her soldiers at all times.

Joan was formally admonished by the court. The next day, she was taken out to the churchyard of the abbey for public condemnation. She was allowed to receive the sacraments despite the court process requiring they be denied to heretics.

After her death, her remains were thrown into the Seine River.

The verdict was a foregone conclusion.

The trial was thought to be unfair and politically motivated.

During the 1450s, her conviction was posthumously investigated on appeal. Her family, particularly her elderly mother, had requested it to clear her name. The appeal was authorized by Pope Callixtus III. The court declared Joan innocent. They declared that Joan had been tried as a result of 'false articles of accusation'.

Joan of Arc has been declared the patron saint of France. She is honored as a defender of the French nation for her role in the siege of Orléans and her insistence on the coronation of Charles VII of France during the Hundred Years' War. Joan was beatified in 1909 and canonized as a virgin, rather than a Christian martyr, in 1920. Joan has been described as an autonomous woman who challenged traditions of masculinity and femininity to be heard as an individual in a patriarchal culture. She set her own course.

Section 2.3
Mary Read and Anne Bonny

There have been many versions of the movie *Treasure Island* based on Robert Louis Stevenson's novel. It was first filmed in 1912. The 1934 version was the first talkie of the book starring Wallace Berry. Think of all the other famous actors who played Long John Silver. They included Orson Welles (1972), Charlton Heston (1990), Jack Palance (1999), Eddie Izzard (2012), and Robert Newton (1950).

Newton was a great British character actor. He was remembered for his portrayal in the 1950 movie and its sequel in 1954. Tim Curry was in *Muppet Treasure Island* (1996). He was surrounded almost entirely by non-human characters, and he was flamboyant and outsized. He played it up.

Douglas Fairbanks starred in the silent *The Black Pirate* in 1926. Many believe that's when pirate films came into their own. Fairbanks performed his own stunts and fenced gracefully. *Captain Blood* (1935), based on a 1922 novel, made a star out of Errol Flynn.

The same is true for those who played Captain Hook in a Peter Pan movie. There were Dust Hoffman (1991) and Ian McShane (2007). In a small role as a voice *in Shrek the*

Third, Cyril Ritchard played Hook next to Mary Martin in the Broadway musical beginning in 1955, and J.K. Simmons, too, was in a stage production. Christopher Walken was on television (2014); Stanley Tucci (2015) was in a British version; and so was Jude Law (2023).

Geena Davis was a pirate in *Cutthroat Island* (1995). With its troubles and chaotic production involving numerous rewrites, this one was probably better forgotten or ignored.

And then there's Johnny Depp as Captain Sparrow. He started with *The Curse of the Black Pearl* (2003) and has reprised the role, for which he is famous many times.

What do these all have in common? They all involve pirates! The Golden Age of Piracy was between the 1650s and the 1730s. It was the third of three phases. The Buccaneering period was the first phase. During this phase, Anglo-French seamen based in Jamaica attacked Spanish colonies.

The second phase, The Pirate Round, was associated with long-distance routes from the Americas to the Indian Ocean and Red Sea. Novels and movies certainly influenced the way in which pirates are thought of and their presumed proclivity for burying treasure and marking the treasure with an 'X' on secret maps. Still, it is the 1950 movie that gave us mages and language that we will never forget.

As for language, some still popular expressions include: 'Shiver me timbers', which expresses surprise. If a big storm is coming, 'Batten down the hatches' is appropriate. Then watch out for the ever-flying 'Jolly Roger' with its crossbones and skull. When playing, don't children still command others to 'walk the plank'?

There were famous real-life pirates, too. Some were executed, such as William 'Captain' Kidd, William Fly, Calico Jack Rackham, and Charles Vane. Captain Kidd is interesting, as he had received a royal commission to hunt down pirates and enemy French ships in the Indian Ocean. When the political climate changed, he was denounced as a pirate. He was arrested and sent to stand trial in England, where he was hung. The belief that he had buried treasure led to many treasure hunts.

Calico Jack Rackham, although a minor captain, was known for having not one, but two female pirates on his crew. Once he was captured and stood trial, the word was out, and it created a media sensation.

Others became legendary. Edward Teach, better known as Blackbeard, had a fierce appearance. His nickname came from his thick black beard, in which it was reported that he tied lit fuses under his hat to scare his enemies. At other times, it was braided into pigtails and sometimes tied with colored ribbons. It did not matter, as he was quite tall with a very scary demeanor.

Despite his efforts, he did not like violence. He and some of his crew were killed by a small group of sailors sent by the governor of Virginia. He was shrewd and calculating and romanticized after his death, but there are no verified accounts of his ever having murdered those he had captured.

There are others. Edward Low was never captured. He was notorious for torturing his victims before he killed them. Henry Morgan was knighted and became governor of Jamaica although he was supposed to be executed. Bartholomew 'Black Bart' Roberts was very successful, becoming the popular subject of novels, films, and video games. Captain Sam Bellamy, also called 'Black Sam' thought of himself as the Robin Hood of pirates. He was merciful and generous.

It really was not that much fun being a pirate. Seafaring was historically regarded as a male activity. Women were rarely allowed on board. Pirates spent a long time at sea— months and months. There were no board games or videos, but there were dice and cards.

Pirates always had to be on the lookout for government ships to avoid capture, which often resulted in public execution. Food was a problem. Food poisoning and malnutrition were not uncommon. There was little variety and disappeared quickly. Without refrigeration, it was difficult to preserve.

Typically, a pirate's life was short-lived, having to overcome illness, starvation, dehydration, battles, and other pirates. Hygiene was very poor. Exposure to the elements could be dire. Captain Kidd was a pirate until he was fifty-four years old, becoming the oldest active pirate during the Golden Age of Piracy. With so many occupational hazards, most only lived into their middle thirties.

Still, there were wonderful places to recuperate, most of them islands in warm climates. Islands had bays and inlets where ships had anchorage. There was also the Carolinas, a favorite spot of Blackbeard who had a house there and sometimes socialized with the governor of the northern state. There was little government in North Carolina, so it became a refuge for outlaws. South Carolina had a shallow coastline, making it difficult for man-of-war ships, but easy for smaller, shallow-draft pirate ships.

Port Royal in Jamaica, considered the pirate capital of the world, was not always a safe haven although it suited thieves and prostitutes, as well as pirates, and it attracted wealth and trade. It was often called the wickedest harbor in the Caribbean. And then there was a devastating earthquake and tsunami in 1692.

Henry Morgan launched his biggest campaign from Port Royal. The British crown had given permission to pirates to go after Spanish shipments on sea and land, so his crew sacked the Spanish City of Panama. This with other attacks earned Morgan a knighthood and political power. He died a rich man.

Although the majority of pirates in history have been men, there are around a hundred known examples of female pirates, about forty of whom were active in the Golden Age of Piracy. Often they had secondary roles, such as smuggling and money lending. The best-known female pirates were Anne Bonny and Mary Read, both of whom were part of Calico Jack's crew, and Rachel Wall. Wall was an American, possibly the first American female pirate and the last to be hanged in Massachusetts. She is discussed earlier in Part I.

Bonny and Read, who was about twelve years older than Bonny, had a strong friendship. Together, they took part in the attacks on merchant vessels. It has been said that the two women fought with more skills and gusto than anyone else on the ship. They both cursed considerably. They were willing to do anything that was asked of them. At first, Read revealed that she was a woman to Bonny and then to Calico Jack. Finally, they were brought to trial together when they were both pregnant.

Their stories are similar but different. No one knows what was true and what wasn't. Bonny was the illegitimate daughter of a lawyer and a serving girl. Her father was so taken with her that he insisted that she live with him, rather than her mother. To avoid a scandal, he dressed her as a boy.

Anyone who asked was told that he wanted to train his offspring as a lawyer's clerk. In Carolina, Anne married a penniless seaman, disappointing her father. She later became the common-law wife of Calico Jack.

Read's mother dressed her as a boy to get money from her rich mother-in-law. Her father had gone to sea and never returned. Read kept running away from wherever her mother placed her, as she didn't like the discipline or the marching, and developed a taste for piracy. She joined Calico Jack's crew after leaving her husband and her ship, on which she was a passenger.

In 1720, Read joined up with Calico Jack on his small ship. It was not a good year for the captain and his crew, as they were captured, went on trial for piracy, and hanged after being found guilty. At the time, both women were pregnant. Some say that Read died in prison from fever, but that Bonny, who had had a little girl, was let go, and was never seen again.

Both Read and Bonny dressed as men when they were involved in acts of piracy. This meant baggy trousers or breeches, a cap, and a billowing linen shirt, just like their fellow seamen. The loose pants, usually cut off at the knee could easily be rolled up for swabbing the deck, wading ashore, or climbing rigging. Tall boots were prized by all.

While clothing had to last and be practical, more extravagant outfits were acquired from passengers on captured ships. These were perfect for a night on the town. When not fighting or pillaging, Read and Bonny wore contemporary women's clothing.

There were other female pirates. One of the earliest was Teuta of Illyria, who was also a queen. With her husband, King Agron, who died in 231 BC, they oversaw hardcore pirates, antagonized the Spartans, led armies and navies that conquered cities and islands along the Adriatic coast, and fought with the Romans. She then went out in a blaze of glory by hurling herself off a mountain after reportedly burying 6,000 pounds of gold in a secret location at a place called Devil's Island.

Maria Lindsey and her husband Eric Cobham in the early eighteenth century practiced piracy for almost twenty years in the Gulf of St. Lawrence, from their base in Newfoundland. Supposedly, they were ruthless, as they used survivors of other ships for target practice. There is no proof that they really existed.

Operating in America during the nineteenth century, Sadie Farrell, known as Sadie the Goat, was a New York gang leader and river pirate on the Hudson and Harlem Rivers. She earned the name 'Queen of the Waterfront'. Or, is this folklore?

Section 2.4
Deborah Sampson

Deborah Sampson was the first American female combat veteran. She is the matriarch of women in the military of the United States, long before Congress formally established the Army Nurse Corps in 1901. Although nurses served in George Washington's army during the Revolutionary War, they were not nurses in the modern sense. Still, they served.

Sampson enlisted in the Continental Army under the name of an older brother, Robert Shurtliff, who had passed away at the age of eight, just before she was born. He was the oldest of Deborah's many brothers and sisters. They were of good Puritan stock and lived in the Massachusetts Bay Colony. It was her second attempt at enlisting.

While her early life was not remarkable, it was difficult. She was born into a rural farming family. Farm life was pure drudgery. Her father struggled but then left when she was five years old. Her mother was unable to provide, so she placed the older children in the households of friends and relatives, a common practice at the time.

When she was eight, Deborah was an indentured servant to a farmer with a large family for ten years. Upon reaching her eighteenth birthday, she had fulfilled the contract to the farmer, and she was 'masterless' or without a master. While indentured, she somehow managed to learn to read although she was not sent to school, as her master did not believe in educating women. She earned her living when released from servitude as a school teacher during summer sessions, which she liked a great deal, and a weaver in the winter for a couple of years.

Deborah was not paid when she was an indentured servant. This was not unusual. It was a form of labor where an individual was under contract to work to repay an indenture or loan within a certain timeframe.

In addition to the hard labor, indentured servants were often subject to violence or physical punishment at the hands of their masters. Female servants might be raped, but they were housed, clothed, and fed. They could also move about locally as long as the work got done. They could marry with permission from the master, but getting married was not on Deborah's mind. She wanted to travel and adventure, to be the equal of any boy.

Most female indentured servants were assigned domestic duties. These included food preparation that was very time-consuming as farm animals needed to be slaughtered, plucked, cooked, and preserved. Produce needed to be planted, tended, harvested, and prepared. Making soaps and candles, churning butter, mending, and washing clothes were other responsibilities.

Women, indentured or not, were expected to get married, have children, and work in the home. They were second-class citizens, subject to their fathers from birth and later handed over to their husbands. Women had the responsibility for sewing—of clothing, bedding, and linens.

Most households lacked the tools to produce their own fabric.

Knitting was usually the first sewing task learned. The tools for knitting were cheap. Mothers taught their daughters how to read, so they could learn the Bible. Girls were not taught to write as it would have required the family to purchase paper.

Although willful and impertinent when a child, for which she was punished, Sampson also had woodworking skills and mechanical ones that included light carpentry, such as producing milking stools and winter sleds. She was also experienced with fashioning wooden tools and implements.

Being respectable was Victorian society's premier virtue. Society valued discipline, grace, and self-control. A woman's reputation was immensely important. Puritans, in particular, had much respect for order and conformity. A typical Puritan woman would have worn well-fitting clothes, in dark shades of red, green, and brown. Her head was usually covered with a cap or bonnet. Brightly colored ribbons were used on the sleeves.

There was much regional variation. New England was influenced by the Puritans who preferred to dress conservatively.

The ideal female figure was strong and shapely, but equally important was excellent posture. The way a woman carried herself was a sign of health, class, and etiquette. Women wore long skirts, which were not practical. Not only were they a fire hazard, but they also collected dirt when in the gardens or just out walking.

On the other hand, with their many layers of material, they provided warmth. It was a time when women were not supposed to be involved in politics. Still, Deborah was very patriotic and wanted to serve her young country.

As Sampson noted, a young woman dared not walk out on the roads to explore and have adventures—even in the early morning. A young woman alone in the world was vulnerable and had to be constantly on guard. "I had known this for I had been a child on my own." So she discovered clothes belonging to a young man about her size. She fashioned an undergarment of firm linen to compress her small breasts. It buckled in the back. Then she had the freedom for which she yearned.

Deborah was tall, about five feet seven or eight inches, and strong from years of hard labor. She was not thin, but taller than the average male. She had fair hair, deep blue eyes, and ivory skin. With plain features, she had no hair on her face, so she looked younger than she was.

Before enlisting, she knew she had to study the behavior of men, so she could imitate it. She had to relearn everything—walking, sitting, bending, drinking, use of arms, and hands, as well as talking. She had to stop curtseying, which had become routine.

Once in the army, she received her regimental coat of dark blue linen. It had white trim on the coat's lapels and a white lining. Her waistcoat and breeches were of white linen. Her square-toed black leather boots had buckles. These were worn with white wool stockings. She also had a light, infantry hat with a black plume tipped in red on one side and a variegated black and white Union cockade on the other. It made her feel brave.

In winter, Sampson wore woolen breeches and a buckskin waistcoat, like others. Her socks were made of thick wool. It was very cold. For insulation, dry leaves were useful.

She lived with five others in a tent, reading them the news of the war. Bathing was always risky. But she knew that if she was alert and aware, she was safe. Still, she always feared that she would be discovered and whipped, jailed, or sent home in shame.

No one suspected that she was a woman. She was often exhausted from fighting, but she did great work, unwilling to be outdone by the men in the trenches. She took part in a series of raids, battles, sieges, and skirmishes. She was thought highly of by the men with whom she fought although one noted that "he fights like a tiger though he looks a bit of a sissy."

On the battlefield, she received a gash in her forehead from a sword and was shot in her left thigh. She extracted the pistol ball without anesthesia herself to avoid the field hospital, where her true identity surely would have been revealed.

When an illness, a fever, later in the year 1783 led to her regiment's doctor learning her secret, he moved her to his house, where she was cared for by his wife and daughters until she was to be discharged at the end of the war. She had always wanted an honorable discharge.

Peace came in September 1783. She was honorably discharged from the army at West Point later.

After the war, she was tired of being someone else. She began dressing appropriately, married, and had several children. She was a typical farmer's wife. Several years later, she published a semi-fictional narrative of her time as a cross-dressed Revolutionary soldier, as she wanted to gain public attention for a military pension. This was awarded to her in 1816 with the help of Paul Revere, who wrote to her district's congressman on her behalf.

A few years earlier in 1802, she began public speaking—she was the first woman lecturer in the country. She did not explain why she had made the choices she did, nor did she glorify traditional female roles. Near the end of her presentation, she returned in her uniform and executed complicated and physically taxing twenty-seven military drills. She consciously refused to be cast firmly in either role. The presentation was very popular.

Sampson's husband petitioned Congress for a pension as the spouse of a veteran. This was granted four years after Sampson death in 1827, as there were no other examples of female 'heroism, fidelity, and courage'. He was awarded a pension, but he sadly died before he could receive any portion of it.

Section 2.5
Sarah Edmonds

Although the wars were different, there are many similarities between the stories of Deborah Sampson during the Revolutionary War and Sarah Emma Edmonds during the Civil War. They both grew up on the family farm. Although Edmonds' father abused her, saying he had wanted a boy to help with the crops, Sampson's father left when she was five. Edmonds' mother insisted on an education for her children.

Edmonds, like Sampson, loved reading. They were both wounded on and off the battlefield, but they feared their disguise would be discovered. Their fellow soldiers spoke highly of them. After the wars, they married and had children. They both wrote their memoirs and gave lectures.

Similar to Sampson, Edmonds easily changed her appearance. She still needed to act the part, as well. It was probably easier for her than other young ladies as she had grown up on a farm and she had not had to learn (and unlearn) how ladies move and sit as most city girls had been taught. She was used to walking through forest and across fields in long, loping athletic strides and riding astride, rather than side saddle.

Edmonds was clever and daring, as well as energetic and adventurous, seeking out physical challenges. She posed as a young man for many years. She enjoyed the freedom to go where she wanted, to do what she wanted, and to earn as much as she could. Canadian-born, her first job in the United States was selling bibles door-to-door. Her boss said that she was the best salesperson he had had in thirty years in business.

At fifteen, to avoid an arranged marriage to an older man, she ran away to live and work with a family friend, making ladies' hats. Her father tracked her down and demanded that she return home. Instead, Edmonds adopted her male persona and disappeared.

Although Canadian by birth, Edmonds felt that it was her duty to serve her new country. She was devoted to the Union cause but always remained a Canadian through and through.

Edmonds was slim and muscular, more handsome than beautiful. Her alias, Franklin Flint Thompson, also enabled her to travel more easily. Similar to Sampson, she was raised to work hard which made her strong. Also, she had a variety of male skills, as well as a gift for mimicry.

Edmonds cropped her long, thick hair, donned a uniform, and became a soldier in the American Civil War. Once in the Union Army, the prevailing standards of male modesty and hygiene during the Victorian Age helped her. Sleeping fully clothed and bathing in undergarments were common among Civil War soldiers in the field. The heavy cloth uniforms, which were generally poor fitting, were perfect to hide a woman's shape. Shunning the foul-smelling, open-trench pits that passed for latrines, many sought the privacy of nearby woods and freshwater streams to attend to their personal needs. Edmonds did not attract attention by doing the same.

Handy with firearms and at home with horses and mules, Edmonds was just what the Union Army wanted. So long as the candidates weren't blind, lame, missing limbs, or subject to fits, they were welcome.

After enlisting, Edmonds was instructed to disguise herself as a slave. She made her skin darker with silver nitrate. Her skin peeled and blistered from the solution. It was assumed to be from a nasty sunburn. Resourceful as usual, she also shaved her head and donned a plantation suit and a curly black wig. She easily passed into the Confederate camp as a slave answering to the name of 'Cuff'.

Silver nitrate was common in medical facilities for treating soldiers. It was used to help treat venereal disease, eye infections, skin ulcers, and infected wounds. It was used topically through the 1800s. Its use declined with antibiotics following World War II.

Venereal disease, as in all wars, was a major problem. It disabled the soldier, decreasing his effectiveness in a fight. It was more frequent near cities.

Edmonds was not the only woman who disguised herself as a man to fight in the Civil War. Historians estimate that 1,000 women did this to serve in either the Union or Confederate Army. Others estimate that four hundred to seven hundred fifty women disguised themselves to fight. When not hiding in plain sight, they did many other things, such as providing blankets, mending shoes, sewing uniforms, washing clothes, and cooking. They also provided medical care for the sick and wounded.

During the Civil War, most professional nurses were men. Men were detailed as nurses. This meant that they were privates assigned to be nurses on a temporary basis for a week or a month to deliver nursing care in the hospital or on the battlefield. They had no training in nursing. That changed after the war when nursing became a public profession, and the women who had served as nurses during the war forged that path for women who came later.

Abolitionist Clara Barton, of course, is the most famous Civil War nurse, and she deserves to be. She became known as the 'Angel of the Battlefield' and went on to found the American Red Cross. She supplied her own wagon and drove out to the field of battle to tend to wounded soldiers. She did this without any permission, but she was so successful and the rate of soldiers returning to duty, who had been under her care, was so great, that she was later authorized to be on the field of battle wherever she could get to it. She risked her life.

A disguise was most often found out if the soldier was wounded and sent to the field hospital where they were discovered by the nurses or the doctors. Clara Barton was said to have discovered a few women soldiers.

There was a desperate need for medical workers. Women began to volunteer as nurses for the wounded. They flocked to this profession because of their inherent capacity to care for another human being. Nurses are often seen as caring, compassionate, patient, and understanding, as are women. In providing medical care, the women nurses comforted and fed patients, wrote letters, and prayed. They managed supplies and staffed hospital kitchens and laundries.

The tasks of a nurse were both physically and mentally challenging. Most women had never experienced a military hospital before and faced a steep learning curve once they had encountered wounded soldiers. For some women, their experiences were emotionally draining. No previous training was required to be a nurse. For the most part, women had learned nursing from their mothers.

Women went to war for the same reasons as men. They wanted to be paid. They also had a strong feeling of patriotism, and they wanted to abolish (or keep) slavery. Some were looking for adventure or to stay close to loved ones.

Women who stayed at home also had big responsibilities. They took over businesses and the running of farms. This meant planting crops on time and getting crops out of the field during the season.

In 1872, the first hospital nursing school in the United States opened. It was based on the standards developed by Florence Nightingale, the founder of modern nursing. She emphasized the benefits of training for nurses during the 1850s Crimean War. She helped establish nursing as a profession in Britain.

Throughout the US Civil War, Nightingale was frequently consulted about how to best manage field hospitals.

After the Civil War, women continued to work in medicine. By 1900, they represented ninety-one percent of US nurses. Army surgeons and other staff were not always happy to see women in what they considered their domain, even when they needed workers. Surgery was not part of medical training. Instead, similar to nurses during the war, they learned to operate on the job.

Edmonds had many disguises. In addition to the slave outfit described earlier, she was also an Irish peddler woman, after procuring proper clothing, as well as several baskets and wares as part of her costume. Her mother had been an Irish immigrant, so she knew the lingo. The ruse worked, and she was allowed behind enemy lines. She also pretended to be a detective and a Southern sympathizer named Charles Mayberry. This, too, put her where she wanted to be.

Edmonds first served as a nurse. She believed that she had the 'gift of nursing', and she pitched in to help at a field hospital. She claimed to have been a spy, but historians dispute the validity of some of her claims. She also was appointed as a regimental mail carrier, which made her very popular with the troops. This meant that she often rode for her life between enemy and friendly lines.

Still, she had lots of freedom for a private. She even had her own horse. As a field nurse, she dealt with mass casualties, especially at Antietam which is known as one of the bloodiest battles of the Civil War although there is no official record of it.

Before the end of the war, in 1863, Edmonds contracted malaria when she had an accident. She was thrown into a ditch and broke her leg, delivering mail. Doctors urged her to go to the hospital for treatment. Instead, she applied for leave, which was denied.

Not wanting to be found out, she put on a disguise and disappeared. It was very mysterious. She checked herself into a private hospital, intending to return to military life once she had recuperated. The disease eventually forced her to give up her military career as she was listed as a deserter.

Malaria is an ancient disease, with prehistoric origins. It is serious and sometimes fatal, causing high fevers, terrible chills, and a flu-like illness. It is carried by mosquitoes that feed on humans. It is curable if diagnosed and treated promptly and correctly.

At first, it was effectively treated with the bark of a tree, which contained quinine. In the early twentieth century, mosquito control measures, such as swamp drainage, covering the surface of open water sources, and screens on windows helped. It was rampant among US troops in the South Pacific during World War II. By 1951, malaria was considered eliminated from the United States.

Section 2.6
Calamity Jane

Calamity Jane was a storyteller, often telling stories about herself that were not true, but they were good for publicity. So, too, was the love of her life, Wild Bill Hickock. He, too, told stories.

Calamity Jane was born Martha Jane Cannary in 1852. She is described as a frontierswoman and sharpshooter. She was a daredevil, and she often wore men's clothing.

Calamity exhibited compassion for the sick and needy. When smallpox hit Deadwood, where she was living, she nursed many back to health.

Jane's mother died of pneumonia when the family was moving West. Her father, who was a gambler, but who had taken up farming, died a year later. There wasn't much she could do about it, but she took responsibility for her five brothers and sisters, taking whatever jobs she could find. She worked as a dishwasher, cook, waitress, dance hall girl, nurse, ox team driver, and occasional prostitute.

She was simply a notorious character, dissolute and devilish, but possessed a generous streak that made her popular.

It is said that she acquired the nickname 'Calamity' when she told men who had offended her that they were 'courting calamity'. Like so much else, it is not known if this were true.

She wrote an autobiographical pamphlet in 1896 for publicity, but her legend is so entwined with the legend of the Old West that it is very difficult to separate fact from fiction.

One of her many claims was that she worked as a scout for General Custer, putting on the uniform. Supposedly, this is when she began dressing as a man. During a march, she swam the Platte River for ninety miles at top speed to deliver important information. She became ill afterward and was forced to spend time recuperating.

Joining a wagon train heading north to Deadwood in 1876, she met Wild Bill Hickok. They became good friends, as they were both heavy drinkers.

From Deadwood, Jane reported that she worked as a Pony Express rider carrying the mail about fifty miles. Her route was over one of the roughest trails in the Black Hills country. She was felt to be a fearless rider.

In Cheyenne, Wyoming by 1869, she learned to cuss, play cards, drink like a fish, and shoot like a cowboy. She was considered a very good markswoman.

James Butler Hickok was born in 1837. He is better known as Wild Bill Hickok. He is often described as a folk hero of the Old West, a soldier, scout, lawman, cattle rustler, gunslinger, showman, and actor.

Hickok was in the country's first public one-on-one quick draw duel, in which he squared off against Davis K. Tutt in 1865. The argument was over gambling debts or maybe a woman when Tutt seized a prized gold, an old pocket watch of Wild Bill's as collateral. Hickok killed Tutt in a way reminiscent of dime novels, radio dramas, and Western movies. Hickok was tried for manslaughter, but he was set free when the jury determined it was a fair fight. Ironically, the two had once been friends although Tutt had fought for the Confederacy and Hickok had fought and spied for the Union Army.

Hickok also knew or, at least, had met Buffalo Bill, General Custer, and Wyatt Earp. He had an imposing presence, aided by two handsome ivory-handled revolvers he always carried. He was a military policeman and then a US Marshal. He did not win reelection as sheriff in Kansas as his methods were too extreme. His first attempt at law enforcement had only lasted three months.

Wild Bill Hickok was the most feared gunfighter in the West.

Deadwood was named by early settlers after the dead trees found in a nearby gulch The town became known for its lawlessness. Murders were common. Justice for murders was not always fair and impartial. The town attained further notoriety when gunman Wild Bill Hickok was killed in 1876 while playing poker. The town's peak was between 1876 and 1879 after gold deposits had been discovered there, leading to the Black Hills Gold Rush. At its height, the town had a population of 25,000. Today it is a National Historic Landmark.

Deadwood, however, was not recognized as 'the wickedest city of the West' although it was one of the liveliest mining camps. That honor goes to Dodge City, known for its gun-slinging and lawlessness, especially in its early years. As buffalo hunters, drifters, railroad workers, and soldiers arrived, they found the many saloons, gambling houses, and brothels to their liking. Differences were settled on the main street with guns.

Deadwood Dick is a fictional character who appears in a series of stories, or dime novels, published between 1877 and 1897 by Edward Lytton Wheeler. The name, Deadwood Dick, became widely known in its time. It was during a period when the country was fascinated by the Black Hills region of the American West after Custer's defeat at Little Bighorn. Wheeler had never been to the Black Hills. The author mixed fictional characters with real-life personalities, such as Calamity Jane and Sitting Bull. He created around one hundred novels.

Calamity Jane was an important character in Wheeler's series of dime novels, beginning with her first appearance in the first issue of the series. Wheeler's series and the character Deadwood Dick was based on a real-life cowboy, named Nat Love. Love was a black cowboy who was born into slavery. Despite regulations, his father taught him to read and write, and he wrote and published his autobiography in 1907 whether true or not. He left home in 1869 to find a better life. It is not clear if he found it.

From Dodge City, Love fought cattle rustlers and endured inclement weather. Training himself, he became an expert marksman. He claimed to have won the rope throw and tie, bridle, saddle, and bronco riding contests although there were no reports of the rodeo in Deadwood newspapers.

In his autobiography, he also claimed to have met Pat Garrett, Bat Masterson, and Billy the Kid among others on cattle drives. He said that he was captured by Indians, who let him go because they respected his heritage.

After marrying, settling down, and moving to Los Angeles, he passed away when he was sixty-six years old.

Almost two decades after Wild Bill was killed, Calamity Jane appeared in Buffalo Bill's Wild West show.

In 1883, Buffalo Bill Cody founded his Wild West Show, an outdoor attraction that toured annually. The show contained a lot of action including wild animals, trick performances, and theatrical reenactments. It was spectacular.

Today, Wild West shows can be found at festivals, rodeos, historic events, and county or state fairs. They are also a regular feature in Old Western Towns, such as Tombstone Arizona. Tombstone's Wild West shows are quite popular with tourists.

Features such as the Pony Express, the wagon train, or the attack on the stagecoach recreated specific and well-known events. Skill acts such as sharp shooting (with pistol and rifle), wing shooting (with a shotgun), roping, and riding not only showcased star performers, but they were also well-received.

In yesteryear, that's where Calamity Jane came in. She had the reputation for being able to handle a horse better than most men. And she could shoot, so she performed sharpshooting astride her horse. She brought the Wild West to the crowds as she had lived it.

But she was still drinking. She had started young, and she had never quit. She was frequently fired for drunkenness and rehired. In 1901, after being hired by the Pan American Exposition for a good salary, she lost her job and was chased out of the town for drunkenness, cursing, and being disruptive.

Hickok had married an older woman by the name of Agnes Lake Thatcher, a fifty-year-old circus proprietor, who had been chasing him around the country for years. Patiently, she waited for him to tire of his long string of female companions. Hickok left his new bride after a few months. Bill explained to her that he was headed to the western goldfields to make a grubstake and would send for her later. She would never see him again.

Hickok attempted to lead a quiet, reasonably respectable life in Deadwood, but his two greatest failings, gambling and liquor, led him into the rough saloons lining the main street of the narrow gulch. By the time he was almost 39, he was going bald and wearing glasses.

Hickok was murdered when he was playing poker at thirty-nine years old in 1876. His back was to the saloon door as his usual seat was taken. He was holding black aces and eights, now known as the Dead Man's Hand—the hole card is unknown. Jane claimed that her guns were at her residence, so she went after his murderer with a meat cleaver.

After Hickok died, Calamity Jane was restless. She left Deadwood the following year and moved around quite a bit. She went to California but left for Texas where she married. Together, Jane and her husband went to Colorado. During the next three years, the family traveled through Wyoming, Montana, Idaho, Washington, Oregon, and South Dakota.

To make ends meet, Jane posed for pictures and sold postcards of herself in her buckskin get-up.

In the summer of 1903, Jane went to Deadwood for the last time. In the final stage of alcoholism and carrying her few belongings in a dilapidated old suitcase, she worked as a cook and laundress in a brothel. She died in August 1903, from inflammation of the bowels and pneumonia.

Hickok was first buried in the Ingelside Cemetery, Deadwood's original graveyard. Almost the entire town attended the funeral. He was later moved to Mount Moriah Cemetery. Per Jane's last wish, she was buried next to Wild Bill, as a posthumous joke on Hickok by the men who had planned her funeral. Her funeral was the largest to be held in Deadwood for a woman.

While Calamity Jane has passed away, she is not forgotten. So many actresses have played her in the movies, including Jean Arthur, Sally Payne, Francis Farmer, and Jane Russell. The same is true of Wild Bill Hickok. Actors who stepped into the role include William S. Hart, Gary Cooper, Charles Bronson, and Jeff Bridges. Both historical figures of the Wild West are featured on television, in plays, games, comics, and literature.

In addition to Jane and Hickok, Wyatt Earp, best-known for being a lawman, and his brother Morgan visited Deadwood. The famous Earps visited Deadwood in the fall of 1876. The two had an interest in the gold rush but didn't end up staying in Deadwood very long.

Bat Masterson also went to Deadwood, Dakota Territory, for the gold rush, but he found more financial success at the gambling tables. He met Wyatt Earp there, who became his lifelong friend.

Section 2.7
Charley Parkhurst

Charley Parkhurst was one of the greatest stagecoach drivers of the Old West during the gold rush days.

Born Charlotte Parkhurst in 1812, she was abandoned by her parents. It is believed that she ran away from an orphanage when she was twelve years old dressed as a boy, as she believed that boys have a great advantage over girls in the battle of life. She found work cleaning out horse stables. She also found a mentor who taught her how to handle horses and drive a coach, first with one, then four, and eventually six horses. She had a special rapport with horses.

She stayed on the East Coast and then went West, like so many others seeking their fortune following the 1849 Gold Rush, in her late thirties. She was charitable and helped those in need. She quickly earned a reputation for her ability to move passengers and gold safely through perilous routes between mining outposts and major towns like San Francisco and Sacramento. The job was hazardous and not for the faint of heart. A historian once described the times as follows: "It was a dangerous era in a dangerous country, where dangerous conditions were the norm." It was certainly no place for a lady, but then, Charley Parkhurst was no lady.

She hauled cargoes of gold through open desert and over steep mountain passes, under constant threat of bad weather, desperados and their hold-up attempts, rattlesnakes, Indians, and grizzly bears. There were also the passengers to be concerned about. And mail. She was considered one of the safest stagecoach drivers. She was not a daredevil, like so many of her contemporaries.

With her fondness for horses, she preferred sleeping in the stable with the horses. Still, she used a whip. She also used the whip to stay out of brawls. Similar to other stagecoach drivers, she was good with a gun. For her skills, she was well paid. She also had a fondness for children, her only feminine trait.

Physically, Parkhurst was very short and stocky, even wiry, with big arms but a high-pitched voice. She wore a black eyepatch, from when a horse, possibly startled by a rattlesnake, kicked her in the face. It made her look tough. She drank whiskey, chewed tobacco, smoked cigars, and swore often. No one knew she was a woman, and she wanted to keep it that way.

She always wore long-fingered beaded gloves, perhaps to hide her small and smooth, feminine hands, in winter and summer, and a pleated shirt to hide a woman's figure. Otherwise, he wore tailored coats, handmade boots, and a broad gray hat.

There was a lot of slang associated with stagecoach driving. Some terms included:

Charlie or whip was a driver; lines or ribbons were used instead of reins; hostlers took care of the horses at stage stops; johnnycake, a type of cornbread, was fed to travelers at stage stops; relay was a team of horses to keep going after a stage stop; and, a road agent was a stagecoach robber.

Some notable stagecoach robbers or road agents had been in prison or were heading there. Charles Boles, one of the most famous, was also known as Black Bart or the Gentleman Bandit. He was always polite and never fired a shot. He robbed twenty-eight stagecoaches between 1877 and 1883. Dick Fellows was another legendary stagecoach bandit.

There is a story about Charley and a road agent with the nickname Sugarfoot. Parkhurst had no patience for the likes of Sugarfoot and his gang. When they demanded that he turn over the 'gold box', Parkhurst cracked his whip and his horses bolted. Turning around, he fired off his revolver. Sugarfoot was no more. He was later found dead with a bullet wound in his stomach. Thanks to Parkhurst.

In appreciation, Wells Fargo gave Parkhurst a watch with a solid gold chain. Wells Fargo took safety seriously.

Gold and other treasures were shipped in sturdy wooden boxes carried in the front of a stagecoach or secured inside the stagecoach in an iron safe.

Travelers had a hard time on stagecoaches. It was not fun. There was the discomfort of close quarters, dusty trails, and lonely stage stations, as well as the threat of Indian attacks and outlaw robbers. The first recorded robbery was in 1856. The last was about 1913. In between, there were 458 robberies.

Still, travelers were required to behave. Smoking and spitting were discouraged. Drinking was allowed, but the drinker was expected to share. Swearing was not allowed, nor was sleeping on a neighbor's shoulder. No one should point out where murders had occurred, especially if women were present.

So why did people take a stagecoach? As roads improved, stagecoaches became faster. Until the late eighteenth century, they had an average speed of about five miles per hour. And, they were relentless, traveling day and night. There were usually four horses although Parkhurst drove six.

In the late 1860s, with the growing popularity of railroads, stagecoach driving became a dying profession. This was noted by Parkhurst, so Parkhurst retired and opened a saloon for a time, as well as worked as a lumberjack in Northern California. In later years, he raised cattle and chickens. It was a quiet life.

During the Civil War, railroads transported troops and supplies, hauled the raw materials for weapons, and actively hired veterans. They were vital for both the Union and Confederate sides.

Before the transcontinental railroad, a trip from the East to the West involved a dangerous trek over rivers, deserts, and mountains. If one were going by sea around Cape Horn, the southernmost tip of Chile where the Atlantic and Pacific Oceans meet, a traveler risked any number of deadly diseases, such as scurvy, rickets, or tetanus. Poor diets only made the situation worse. This, of course, was before the Panama Canal.

The first railroad in the United States began in the 1830s along the East Coast. In the 1840s, there were railroads in the East. Midwest, and South. Interest in going from coast to coast grew. In the 1850s, Congress investigated routes for a transcontinental railroad.

The Union Pacific was founded in 1862. It was created and funded by Congress. Construction was slow due to the Civil War. After the war, veterans and Irish immigrants provided the labor. That same year, the Central Pacific was also started.

Eventually, the Chinese, of which there were about 12,000 laborers, accomplished amazing tasks, living in tunnels as they worked their way through solid granite. Resistance from the Sioux, Cheyenne, and Arapaho who were seeing their homeland changed beyond recognition was fierce. The two railroads inked up in Utah in 1869. It was one of America's greatest technological feats of the century.

Using her secret identity, Charles Darkey Parkhurst was a registered voter over fifty years before the passage of the Nineteenth Amendment. It is often claimed that she was the first woman to vote in a US presidential election although many historians doubt this is true, and there is no evidence. After all, it says so on her gravestone.

No one knew Charley Parkhurst was a woman until she died in 1879. Neighbors, who came to his cabin to lay out the body, discovered what Charley had kept secret her entire life. The examining doctor also noted that Charley had given birth at some time. The discovery was at first a local sensation, and then a national one, especially as no one knew his secret. Even in the nineteenth century, there was admiration for Parkhurst's feat of disguise.

She was sixty-seven years old when she died. She was buried in Watsonville Pioneer Cemetery in Northern California.

Watsonville, a city along the Central Coast of California, is known for its great weather.

There was another Charley. This one had the nickname of Mountain Charley and the last name of Forest. She was born Elsa Jane Guerin in the 1800s and told her story in her self-published memoirs. Elsa Jane had two children whom she loved before she was sixteen, and she learned her husband had been murdered. Since she was left without any resources at all, she decided her best course of action was to pass as a man and get a job. She learned male mannerisms, cut her hair, placed her children with nuns, and found a job as a cabin boy and then a break man on a steamer before she went to California.

Gold prospecting was grueling, and she subsequently found work in a saloon in which she bought half a stake. She also reports that she started a pack-mule freight hauling business and drove a cattle herd. She was not hurting for money.

At one point, she shot a blackguard who blew her cover by announcing that she was a woman. She married again, her bartender, and they moved to Missouri. She collected her children whom she had visited monthly. It is not known what part of her autobiography is true.

Section 2.8
George Sand

George Sand might have lived in the 1800s, but she had modern ideas.

Sand was born in 1804, after the French Revolution. Her birth name was Amantine Lucille Aurore Dupin. Friends called her Aurore.

Sand had a small figure with huge dark eyes that were always beguiling and mysterious. She could walk at ten months, and she was a very good reader by the time she was four.

She was passionate about her writing, her children, and her lovers. She was generous to a fault, supporting various lovers and her children into her old age, paying for her nephew's education, and providing a substantial dowry for her daughter and a poor relative. She fed over forty local peasant families, a gesture that endeared her to her neighbors.

She is best known as the famous lover of the celebrated pianist and composer Chopin.

Sand did many things that were frowned upon at the time, but she was so famous that it hardly mattered. It was not just her cross-dressing that drew attention, but it was also her many lovers, leaving her marriage to write, the subjects of her novels, and her political views. George Sand wore a top hat, trousers, and frock coat in the streets. She claimed that pants and such were less expensive and much sturdier than dresses. Male attire enabled her to circulate more freely and increased her access to venues where women were barred. She was comfortable, even if no one else was.

Sand enjoyed the theater, but she did not have the money for expensive tickets. The Pit, downstairs and cheaper, into which only men were admitted, was just the ticket. She had her tailor make her a riding coat in heavy, gray cloth with a matching waistcoat and trousers. For shoes, she wore metal-heeled boots, so much better than flimsy women's shoes. Then to top it all off, she put on a woolen cravat. And she enjoyed the play and the ones that followed, making up for lost time.

The authorities did not approve of cross-dressing. In 1800, a law was passed that prohibited women from dressing like men in public. To do so, required women to secure authorization based on health reasons and only health reasons. Of course, Sand did not bother with the required permit.

Smoking was a pleasure for Sand at a time when it was completely unacceptable for women. She smoked cigars, for which she is famous, but also cigarettes, which she rolled with deft expertise. She also delighted with her beloved hookah. She became thoroughly dependent on tobacco, much concerned about running out.

She felt soothed by needlework and adored jam-making. Even when doing the latter, she displayed her characteristic tendency to overdo, producing ludicrous quantities.

The union of her parents was, in the eyes of her paternal grandmother, an abomination. She abandoned her plans to annul the marriage when she saw her infant granddaughter, but she persisted in disparaging her 'gutter-snipe' daughter-in-law Sophie. (Her son, Sand's father, had accidentally died when Sand was four.) Sophie and Aurore went to live with her grandmother in the Berry region, but friction between Sophie and Aurore's grandmother compelled Sophie to return to Paris. At some point, she knew that her mother and grandmother would never reconcile.

Sand's mother Sophie was charming but uneducated with a temper, and she led a lifestyle that was deemed 'debauched and wanton' by Sand's grandmother/guardian. Proud of her ancestry and social class, Sand's grandmother resolved to mold and educate Aurore in the role of the well-born heiress she was.

Sand was raised for much of her childhood by her grandmother. When she was thirteen years old, she was strong-willed and often rebellious. Her grandmother, not knowing how to control her, enrolled her in a convent school in Paris. An excellent student, Aurore embraced religion and declared her intention of becoming a nun. Her grandmother put an end to such talk and removed her from school in 1820.

When Aurore was sixteen years old, her grandmother was paralyzed by a stroke, and Aurore returned to the family home to care for her.

When her grandmother died in 1821, Aurore became the center of a family dispute between her father's relatives and her mother over her custody.

Her mother Sophie won the battle, and Aurore moved to Paris, but her mother was increasingly remote. As a child, she had longed to be tucked up close to her mother, and the need for physical closeness never went away. Still, in Paris, she was bored and restless.

When she was eighteen years old, in 1822, as heiress to Nohant and an investment house in Paris, Sand was not without prospects, despite her mother's lower-class origins. Sand married François Casimir Dudevant, nine years her senior. With her marriage, Sand became a baroness although it was a title she never used. She and Dudevant had two children, Maurice and Solange. She left her family and returned to Paris.

The family home was in the village of Nohant, a small village in the rolling hills and rich farmlands of France's Berry region. It is now a two-hour drive from Paris.

The house itself was not quite a chateau—more like a manor house. It was not immense, so one could live in it. Sand and her brood did just that. Sand held court there and wrote novels with astonishing fluency and discipline to support herself, her family, and her generous lifestyle.

The house features a large garden and a small park, with many features and aspects that Sand designed herself. She planted two cedar trees to commemorate the births of her children. There are also a few rooms within the house that Sand designed, including the 'blue room', where she died in 1876.

The house has been preserved because it was where Sand wrote many of her books and hosted some of the most important artists and writers of her time, including Chopin, Liszt, Balzac, Turgenev, and Delacroix. The writer and her family are buried in a small cemetery between the garden and the village church.

After the evening meal, merriment abounded in Nohant's theater. The actors were guests, members of the household, and those who lived nearby. They also made up the audience.

After the festivities, Sand wrote. Sitting at her small desk, she faithfully wrote her twenty or more pages every night, from midnight to 4:00 am.

Sand's life revolved more and more around Nohant rather than Paris. Writers and artists and family and friends created a lively milieu for her creative energies.

From 1837 until her death in 1876, she spent long summers at the house, usually from May until November.

For all of her daring, Sand felt that the bohemian life of Paris was not her authentic milieu. At heart, she was a true French countrywoman.

When she was twenty-seven years old, George Sand adopted the nom de plume George Sand. Sand was based on the last name of her first lover, a law student, Jules Sandeau who was seven years her junior. Their collaboration, *Rose et Blanche*, a novel, was published in 1831. Their affair ended when she noticed that Sandeau lacked her discipline and drive although he envied her production.

Sand's literary legacy includes more than seventy novels in addition to several plays, countless essays, literary criticism, journalistic pieces, and a multivolume autobiography. She wrote daily.

Indiana (1832), her first novel which she wrote by herself, brought her immediate attention. *Valentine* (1832) soon followed. She is best known for her rustic novels, such as *La Mare au Diable* (1846). Their chief inspiration was from her lifelong love of the countryside and her sympathy for the poor.

Lélia (1833), her third novel by herself, received mixed reviews. It called attention to the unequal status of women in society. Sand was accused of advocating free love and other morally dangerous ideas.

George Sand was one of the most popular writers in Europe in the 1800s. She was highly respected by the literary and cultural elite in France.

George Sand lived after the French Revolution which lasted from 1789 until 1799. It changed nearly all aspects of French and European life. Powerful sociopolitical forces were unleashed by a people seeking Liberty, Equality, and Fraternity. Liberal democracy was born.

Some countries wanted to restore the *Ancien Régime* by force. In France, the monarchy was abolished and destroyed. There was an ongoing need for reform.

The next century, the eighteen hundreds, was also quite dramatic. Factions vied for power. Kings needed money. Napoleon abdicated, and his nephew staged a coup. The Bourbon monarchs were restored to the throne. There was a second and a third Republic and a Second Empire.

There was an ongoing struggle for political control, exacerbated by economic depression and civil disorder, but it also served to unify and strengthen France as a country and a people.

Everyone had a point of view or an issue, especially Sand. She wrote about them in her novels. Liberals wanted moderate reform; socialists wanted far-reaching social changes. Sand was a socialist.

After the revolution, the style of Marie Antoinette was gone. Frivolity and excess, as well as large, enormous skirts and hairstyles, were replaced with modest gowns. Simple chemise and tunic dresses, which were high-waisted, were made of soft fabric without boning or padding. There was little corseting.

The body was free to be shown off. Arms were bared, breasts were exposed with very low necklines, and even backs were shown off as they hadn't been before although legs were still covered. The silhouette was tall and vertical.

This was just the beginning, as styles changed again. No wonder Sand preferred men's clothing although there were changes to men's attire, as well. Men wore suits with embroidered silks and laced ruffled collars.

In the mid-century, women's clothing usually was made of silk and embroidered with floral patterns. Half sleeves covered in layers of lace ruffles were in vogue. Necklines were so revealing that some women covered their cleavage with a piece of lace out of modesty. These dresses were usually worn by aristocrats and women of wealth. The waist kept getting smaller, while the skirt got wider and wider and the sleeves got fuller requiring wires to retain their fullness.

Everything was laden with all sorts of trimmings, as well as ribbons and ruffles of lace. Men's fashion was relatively simple; pants were tighter fitting and went down to the knee. Although men's fashion was different during this time period, it was still very detailed.

By the end of the century, both men's and women's styles mellowed out. Dresses became more of a hybrid of the styles from the beginning and the middle of the century. Men wore darker clothes with more conservative collars.

George Sand had intense, platonic relationships, frequently with men younger than herself. She also had a well-known relationship with a woman, actress Marie Dorval. The two met in 1833 after Sand wrote Dorval a letter of appreciation following one of her performances.

She wrote about Dorval, including many passages in her journals, where she described herself as being smitten with Dorval. They certainly had an intimate friendship, but it was only rumors that they were lovers. This has been debated but never verified. Sand was warned to stay away from Dorval. They remained close friends.

Sand had romantic relationships with other authors, painters, playwrights, actors, musicians, composers, and politicians. In later life, such as with Gustav Flaubert, they simply engaged in correspondence. The two were very close.

Frédéric Chopin was possibly George Sand's most famous lover. Their love affair lasted nine years. When they met at a party, she initially repelled him. He remarked, "What an unattractive person *la Sand* is. Is she really a woman?" She, on the other hand, was immediately intoxicated and set out in pursuit. She was often the pursuer, rather than the pursued.

After a year and a half, he was drawn to her personality and celebrity. The two first became friends and then lovers and, for many years, lived close to each other in Paris. They journeyed to Majorca together and encountered terrible weather, and his health, never great, declined.

Chopin was a Polish composer and virtuoso pianist. Once a child prodigy, he supported himself by selling his compositions and giving piano lessons. In Paris, he seldom performed publicly, choosing the intimacy of a salon. His preference was to play in his apartment for small groups of friends.

Within his Paris circle were conductor and composer Hector Berlioz, conductor and composer Ferdinand Hiller, poet and critic Heinrich Heine, painter Eugène Delacroix, poet and writer Alfred de Vigny, and Franz Liszt, among others. His relationship with Liszt was noteworthy. Both were hugely popular and revered, and they displayed admiration for each other although they were so different. Liszt was all flair; Chopin was subtle. When Chopin died, Liszt was heartbroken.

On Majorca, after discovering that Sand and Chopin were not married, the deeply traditional Catholic people of the island became inhospitable, making accommodations difficult to find. The bad weather had such a detrimental effect on Chopin's health that Sand was determined to leave the island. In May 1839, they headed to Sand's estate at Nohant for the summer, where they spent most of the following summers until 1846 during which, without the need to earn money and the distractions of Paris, Chopin composed some of his greatest music. In autumn, they returned to Paris, where Chopin's apartment was close to Sand's. He frequently visited Sand in the evenings, but both retained some independence.

Chopin's health continued to deteriorate. For large parts of his life, Chopin was troubled by respiratory tract infections, severe breathing problems, and loss of weight. It has been thought that he died of tuberculosis. Sand was the one to end the relationship, but they had always loved each other.

As the composer's illnesses progressed, Sand became more of a nurse and less of a lover to Chopin. He died at thirty-nine years old in 1849. George Sand lived another twenty-seven years.

Her last lover was the engraver Alexandre Damian Manceau, to whom her son had introduced her. Manceau gave her both love and friendship, which was unique to her. It was all without drama and lasted fifteen years. He has been described as intelligent, talented, and devoted to her. Sand was at the peak of her career. She was over a decade older than he was, but she outlived him by nine years. She passed away at Nohant in 1876.

George Sand continues to interest us. Although most movies focus on the tumultuous periods of her life, a number of notable actresses have played her, such as Merle Oberon, Patricia Morison, Rosemary Harris, and Judy Davis in a British-American movie. Juliette Binoche was in the 1999 French film *Children of the Century*.

Section 2.9
Isabelle Eberhardt

During her short life, Isabelle Eberhardt was an explorer and writer. She disguised herself as a Muslim man. She dreamed of liberty.

Isabelle's mother was tall, slender, graceful, and gentle. Her father was a Russian of noble birth, a general in the Tsar's Imperial Army. When he died, he left his fortune to his wife. Otherwise, he had a terrible character and was detested by all.

The general brought into the household a tutor. Trophimovsky, the tutor, was of Armenian background with a classic profile and soft dark eyes. He was a scholar who had studied philosophy and knew Latin and Greek. In addition to Russian, he spoke Turkish, Arabic, and German. Still, he had adopted a nihilistic doctrine. Over time, he grew more and more disagreeable and difficult.

The family settled in Switzerland where Isabelle was born illegitimate in 1877. Then her mother and the tutor ran away together, taking Isabelle and her brothers.

Isabelle, slender but not frail, was nearly as tall as her brothers. The tutor never recognized her as his daughter. She wore male clothes because they were practical. They also gave her more security when she went to town. Her hair was cut short.

Her education was as complete as that of her brothers. She could read French, German, Italian, Russian, and Arabic. She learned history and geography, with some philosophy. She enjoyed painting and drawing for which she had talent.

She had soft black eyes, delicate sensual lips, a flat upturned nose, and long fine hands.

Isabelle was urged to have a literary career, to be based on a study of the East and Arab life. With her mother, the two went to Algeria.

At the time, Algeria was a French colony. This situation lasted until the end of the Algerian War, leading to independence in 1962. It was considered a part of France, rather than a colony.

France wanted to put an end to the Barbary pirates and increase the king's popularity among the French people.

Algeria is best known for being filled with legendary landscapes that include perfectly preserved Roman ruins and the Sahara Desert.

In the Casbah, Isabelle smelled the heavy, penetrating smell of kif. The smell intrigued and excited her; she would have liked to share in every custom of the Orient so that she might become really a part of it and forget all about Europe.

Kif or Kef is a substance. It is often called marijuana or cannabis. It is smoked to produce a drowsy state, capable of producing a euphoric condition.

In Islamic countries, women could not wander unaccompanied. Male Arab dress seemed a natural protection. Soon, she was seen in the long, snowy-white burnous and a high-swathed muslin turban. Europeans were horrified. Isabelle did not care.

A burrnous, also burnoose, is a long cloak of coarse woolen fabric with a pointed hood, often white in color, traditionally worn by Arab and Berber men in North Africa. White is the dominant color of a burnous as it is cooler. The Prophet, Muhammad, wore a turban on his head.

Isabelle also had a practical side and lots of ambition. When a local newspaper accepted one of her stories, she filled her diary with documentation, including notes on local customs and word sketches of people or landscapes.

Isabelle's conversion seemed useful. She was completely absorbed by her new life. But she never forgot her mother, even after she had passed away from a heart attack in 1897. Isabelle was twenty years old and an eternal wanderer. She had to keep moving.

In Tunis, both Arabs and Europeans began gossiping about her. Although she practiced the rules of Islam, she drank. This went against the Prophet's rule. The belief was that Muslims should avoid even indirect association with alcohol. She never failed to recite the ritual prayers five times a day. She dressed as a man and could be seen stretched out on a mat, simply dreaming. Often, she let young men make love to her. Agents of the government watched her.

Unfortunately, Isabelle was reckless with her money, as well as her health and reputation. The money her mother had left her ran out. To make a journey, she needed permission from the Arab bureau. She ventured South and became Si Mahmoud. This gave her some protection. She was a nomad in the desert. The endless dunes gave her freedom, losing touch with reality. Returning to Tunisia, she was penniless.

When she was twenty-three, she was totally alone. She made another journey to the South.

The gossip continued, as did her poverty. To feed herself, she pawned her few belongings, thinking she was happy.

She was ordered to leave Algeria by the French administration, but she was allowed to return the following year after marrying her partner, the Algerian soldier, Slimane Ehnni, who was considered to be French.

When she married, she became French and could no longer be excluded from French colonies. She was so excited about the wedding ceremony that she dressed as a woman, even proposing that she wear a wig to cover her short, cropped hair.

When she was twenty-seven, she made her last journey to Algiers. She had been to Switzerland several times to tend to Trophimovsky who was dying, to see her favorite brother, to sell the chateau. She suffered the Europeans among whom she dwelled. They were the infidels.

Returning from a visit to her brother and his wife on a steamship, women were not admitted to the fourth-class deck. Traveling under a man's name, she described herself as a day laborer. No one questioned her.

She became disappointed with her husband, upon realizing that his only ambition after leaving the army was finding an unskilled job that would allow him to live relatively comfortably.

Isabelle and her husband moved to Ténès, a small town in Algeria with bored and spiteful Europeans. Considered a traitor for she was a writer, she could make no move without being observed. She had attacks of fever, probably malaria or maybe syphilis, which left her weak. Her husband, too, was in failing health.

A flash flood destroyed their mud home. A search for her was conducted, and her body was found under one of the house's supporting beams. The exact circumstances of her death were never known.

She always knew she would die young. She was twenty-seven years old.

Section 2.10
Billy Tipton

The 1920s brought so many great things. Gloria Swanson reigned in Hollywood. Babe Ruth ruled on the baseball field and was the unofficial king of New York. Albert Einstein, a famous scientist, developed the theory of relativity. Charlie Chaplin reigned in silent movies while Charles Lindbergh ruled the skies, flying solo across the Atlantic. Amelia Earhart was the first woman to fly solo across the Atlantic. The most important consumer product was the automobile.

Yes, there was a downside. Not everyone benefited. The sale of alcoholic drinks was banned, crime and corruption were rampant, and the Great Depression began in 1929.

The thirties were interesting too. By 1932, one in four American workers was not employed due to the depression. The first technicolor Mickey Mouse short film was released. Superman had his debut in 1938. The Boulder Dam opened two years ahead of schedule.

Good or bad, nothing stopped Billy Tipton. He was born Dorothy Lucille Tipton in Oklahoma City on December 29, 1919, but he lived most of his adult life as a man. It is believed that he started dressing as a man, so he could play jazz in a band, leading the itinerant life of a professional musician, and he never stopped. He never explained his motivation for cross-dressing. Maybe, Tipton wanted travel and adventure.

Tipton was never legally married, but five women called themselves Mrs. Tipton during his life. He locked the bathroom when he washed and dressed. He wore a binding on his chest to support his ribs that had been fractured in a car accident. Or so he said.

He added a jockstrap filled with rolled stockings when his outfits became more complex. There were other cues as to his gender that he hid, including his walk, his speech, his attitude, and never crossing his legs or playing with his hair. Instead, he had careful barbering and oiling. He knew that was equally important to have an attractive female partner. By 1933, he was reborn.

Tipton was a perpetual improviser, and he was never out of character. He thought of himself as an entertainer, who had an artist's pride in craft and discipline. He was also quite a good mimic. An early photo of Tipton shows her black hair slicked back wearing a tie, white shirt, pants, a double-breasted blazer, and boutonniere. Always optimistic about finding work, he spent money on studio portraits.

Tipton understood how to play a role that required pants. Knowing it was largely a man's world, he had to be aggressive at times. He expressed aggression through humor or stony silence. He managed to get clothes to dress as a boy. Only 5'5", but Tipton stood tall enough to look like a man compensating for his short stature. At some point, he put lifts in his shoes.

Tipton adored his parents. He thought they were glamorous, good-looking, and sexy. They were. They were also hot-tempered and ambitious. His mother, Reggie Parks, had been raised in an orphanage where she was the youngest and prettiest girl.

With her long blond curls, she was treated differently than everyone else. His father George William or G.W. worked as a machinist and drove racing cars. When not working, he was something of a playboy. In disguise, Tipton couldn't talk about them or his childhood, as it might give him away.

The family did not accept Tipton's changes.

In 1935, Tipton got his first real job. He went on the road with a band. He played saxophone most of the time, piano some of the time, and a boy all of the time. He was so successful at being male that he had to fend off female advances.

Tipton got along well with everyone. Part of his success in passing was that he was a shrewd observer of the psychology of other people. He looked for common ground.

In 1937, Tipton got a social security card as a man.

The depression was ending in 1939 as the country geared up for war. Tipton needed a draft card and found a doctor who classified him as 4F.

In the late 1940s, the music business was changing. The big band era was over. Tipton, who had made a living impersonating the trendsetters of the times, needed to make a living. He thought about forming a trio or quartet as people still liked his music.

He got a job, but it did not last long. He made a living wherever he could. He also began giving piano lessons.

Then his luck changed, and he joined a thirteen-piece band. After that, he began managing his own trio.

From 1954 through 1958, Tipton gained success as a musician. The trio received good word-of-mouth and recorded two albums of jazz standards for a small record label. He rehearsed his group constantly. He did not want anything to interfere with the music. He wrote out each week such things as who was going to wear what each night. The group could play for a month without repeating clothes. He was very fussy.

Tipton toured around the Midwestern states and into Wyoming, Colorado, and Texas with various bands. He performed for over two years in Joplin, Missouri. Finally, it was time for him to settle down, which he did in Spokane as a booking agent on commission in 1958.

The nightclubs and after-hours spots were for men only. It was like a law of nature. Billy lived a middle-class life. He and his 'wife' adopted children. However, at night, after a nap, he was once again an entertainer.

In the 1970s, Tipton's arthritis got worse, and he became reluctant to play the piano. There were money problems.

By the summer of 1984, Tipton was in debt. He was so nice and generous that he allowed people to take advantage of him.

No matter what, Tipton kept up his appearance. He did not have new clothes or fancy ones, but his shirt was always pressed and tucked in.

A cold caught in 1988 lingered. He looked thin and tired. His health continued to deteriorate.

By the time of his death in 1989, Billy was almost destitute. Untreated, hemorrhaging ulcers finally did him in, as he had refused to go to a doctor, After his death, friends and family were surprised to learn that he was a woman. This information came as a shock to nearly everyone, including the women who had considered themselves his wives, as well as his sons and the musicians who had traveled with him.

More About Kansas City

Kansas City was right in the middle of the United States. It took three hours by plane to reach the East Coast and three hours by plane to reach the West Coast. Transcontinental trips at the time, whether by plane or train, often necessitated a stop in the city. Not to mention, it was hot. It was not one of the cities that influenced the development of jazz, those honors went to New Orleans, Chicago, and New York.

In 1929, Tipton at fourteen years old and her brother at seven were sent to live with two aunts, Bess and Dove, in Kansas City. Bess was bossy and full of adventure. She had married a man of property. Bess and her husband liked the gambling laws that restored horse racing to Kansas City. It was good for business. Dove was mild-mannered and warm.

She, too, had married well. Bess did her best to make Dorothy into a proper young lady. Bess also was responsible for Tipton's training as a musician, enrolling both children at a school of music. Dorothy studied piano, violin, and saxophone.

In Kansas City, although young, Tipton picked up on jazz. Nightspots were open twenty-four hours a day, and they were under police protection. Also, strong female piano players abounded. Dance music and jazz were everywhere—in record stores, on the streets, in fancy hotels, and on the radio.

Count Basie played in Kansas City. Charlie Parker began his ascent to fame in the city which was his hometown in the 1930s.

Kansas City jazz had certain characteristics, such as:

- It was more relaxed than elsewhere.
- It kept going along with the non-stop nightlife. It was a very competitive environment. The goal was to say something with one's instrument.
- The bands usually played by memory, rather than sight-reading. This made the music more spontaneous.
- There was much riffing, which is a short, memorable section of music, usually made up on the spot. It encourages improvisation.

Bibliography

Bronski, M. (2011) *A Queer History of the United States*, Boston: Beacon Press.

Browder, L. (2006) *Her Best Shot: Women, 2008nd Guns in America*, Chapel Hill: University of North Carolina Press.

Cate, C. (1975) *George Sand: A Biography*, New York: Avon Publishers.

Cawthorne, N. (2004) *A History of Pirates: Blood and Thunder on the High Seas*, London: Chartwell Book, Inc.

Cooney, K. (2018) *When Women Ruled the World: Six Queens of Egypt*, Washington D.C.: National Geographic Partners, LLC.

Du Preez, M. and Dronfield, J. (2016) *Dr. James Barry: A Woman Ahead of Her Time*, Great Britain: Oneworld Publications.

Eisler, B. (2006) *Naked in the Marketplace: The Lives of George Sand*, New York: Counterpoint Press.

Gallagher, A. (2021) *New Women in the Old West: From Settlers to Suffragists*, New York.

Gansler, L. (n.d.) *The Mysterious Private Thompson: The Double Life of Sarah Emma Edmonds, Civil War Soldier*, Lincoln: University of Nebraska Press.

Hall, R. (1993) *Patriots in Disguise: Women Warriors of the Civil War*, New York: Paragon House.

Klass, S. S. (2009) *Soldier's Secret: The Story of Deborah Sampson*, New York: Henry Hold and Company, LLC.

Konstam, A. (2002) *The History of Pirates*, USA and Canada: The Lyons Press.

Ledbetter, S. (2006) *Shady Ladies: Nineteen Surprising and Rebellious American Women*, New York: A Tom Doherty Associates Book.

Lee, M. (2018) *Bygone Badass Broads: 52 Forgotten Women Who Changed the World*, New York: Abrams.

León, V. (1995) *Uppity Women of Ancient Times*, New York: MJF Books.

Mackworth, C. (1975) *The Destiny of Isabelle Eberhardt: A Biography*, New York: The Ecco Press.

Markley, B. and Kellen C. (2018) *Old West Showdown: The Mythic Old West*, USA: Globe Pequot.

Mays, D. A. (2004) *Women in Early America: Struggle, Survival, and Freedom in a New World*, Santa Barbara.

McLaird, J. D. (2005) *Calamity Jane: The Woman and the Legend*, Norman: University of Oklahoma Press.

McCurry, S. (2019) *Women's War: Fighting and Surviving the American Civil War*. Cambridge, Massachusetts, and London, England: The Belknap Press of Harvard University Press.

Middlebrook, D. W. (1998) *Suits Me: The Double Life of Billy Tipton*, Boston and New York: Houghton Mifflin Company.

Middleton, D. (1982) *Victorian Lady Travelers*, Chicago: Academy Chicago.

Miller, L. (1984) *On Top of the* World: *Five Women Explorers in Tibet*, Seattle: The Mountaineer.

Monson, M. (2018) *Frontier Grit: The Unlikely True Stories of Daring Pioneer Women*, Salt Lake City: Shadow Mountain Publishing.

Pendergast, S. and Pendergast, T. (2004) *Fashion Costume and Culture Modern World*, Michigan: The Gale Group.

Price, S. D. and Thomas P. McCarthy. Edited and intro by

Stories of the Old West: 44 Great Tales of the American Frontier. An imprint of Globe Pequot. 2018.

Includes My Life and Adventures by Calamity Jane—first published as a pamphlet—about 1883 Signed: Yours, Mrs. M. Burk better known as Calamity Jane

Nichols, J. (2007) *Chopin: His Life and Music*, Naperville: Sourcebooks.

Sams, E. (1995) *The Real Mountain Charley*, Ben Lomond: Yellow Tulip Press.

Salmonson, J. A. (1991) *The Encyclopedia of Amazons*: *Women Warriors from Antiquity to the Modern Era*, New York: Anchor Books/Doubleday.

Seagraves, A. (1996) *Daughters of the West*, Hayden: Wesanne Publications.

Spoto, D. (2007) *Joan: The Mysterious Life of the Heretic Who Became a Saint*, New York: HarperCollins.

Velasco, S. (2018) The *Lieutenant Nun*: *Transgenderism, Lesbian Desire, & Catalina de Erauso*, Austin: University of Texas Press.

Wilson-Smith, T. (2006) *Joan of Arc: Maid, Myth, and History*, Great Britain: Sutton Publishing Limited.

Yolen, J. and Stemple, H. (2013) *Bad Girls: Sirens, Jezebels, Murderesses, Thieves, & Other Female Villains*, Watertown: Charlesbridge.

Magazines:

Editors. (2022) 'Pirate haven of Port Royal: wickedest harbor in the Caribbean', *National Geographic History*, 62–75.

Phillips, B. (n.d.) 'Masking up: European fashion's strange cover story', *National Geographic History*, 16–18.

Toole, T. (2022) 'The appearance of freedom', *National Geographic History*.

Several websites have been consulted to check on spelling, dates, and facts. Of those used most frequently are legends of america.com

america.com|Currated City-Guide of america.com
With more than 2000 listed and verified places including restaurants, attractions and museums, america.com is the go-to place to plan your next trip to the UK.
america.com
Wikipedia.org